why acting matters

Yale

University

Press

New Haven

and

London

David

Thomson

Why

Acting

Matters

Published with assistance from the foundation established in memory of Henry Weldon Barnes of the Class of 1882, Yale College.

Yale University Press books may be purchased in quantity for educational, business, or promotional use. For information, please e-mail sales.press@yale.edu (U.S. office) or sales@yaleup.co.uk (U.K. office).

Set in Times Roman and Adobe Garamond types by Integrated Publishing Solutions.

Printed in the United States of America.

Library of Congress Cataloging-in-Publication Data

Thomson, David, 1941–. Why acting matters / David Thomson.
    pages   cm—(Why X matters)
Includes bibliographical references.
ISBN 978-0-300-19578-1 (cloth : alk. paper)   1. Acting.   I. Title.
PN2061.T525 2015
792.02′8—dc23
2014029867

A catalogue record for this book is available from the British Library.

This paper meets the requirements of ANSI/NISO Z39.48-1992 (Permanence of Paper).

10 9 8 7 6 5 4 3 2 1

Also by David Thomson

The New Biographical Dictionary of Film (sixth edition, 2014; first
    edition, as *A Biographical Dictionary of Film,* 1975)
Moments That Made the Movies (2013)
The Big Screen: The Story of the Movies (2012)
Try to Tell the Story: A Memoir (2009)
*The Moment of Psycho: How Alfred Hitchcock Taught America to Love
    Murder* (2009)
"Have You Seen . . . ?": A Personal Introduction to 1,000 Films (2008)
Nicole Kidman (2006)
The Whole Equation: A History of Hollywood (2004)
In Nevada: The Land, The People, God, and Chance (2001)
Beneath Mulholland: Thoughts on Hollywood and Its Ghosts (1998)
Rosebud: The Story of Orson Welles (1997)
4–2 (1996)
Showman: The Life of David O. Selznick (1993)
Silver Light (1990)
Warren Beatty and Desert Eyes: A Life and a Story (1987)
Suspects (1985)
America in the Dark: Hollywood and the Gift of Unreality (1978)
Wild Excursions: The Life and Fiction of Laurence Sterne (1972)
Hungry as Hunters (1972)
A Bowl of Eggs (1970)
Movie Man (1967)

For Justin, Heather, Carmine, Julia, and Jim

"Scratch an actor," said Laurence Olivier, "and you find an actor."
He should have known, but I don't think it's true, or any more true
of actors than politicians, or priests, or teachers, or strippers, or anyone else engaged in acts of public self-display. What *is* true, I think,
is that if you scratch an actor you will find a child. Not that actors
are inherently less mature than politicians, priests, etc., but actors
must retain a child's appetite for mimicry, for demanding attention, and above all for playing. They must see with a child's heart,
innocent of judgement.

RICHARD EYRE, *Utopia and Other Places*

They were waiting to go on, and I heard them say: "Where did you
have lunch today, old boy?—Oh, Rules. Where did you?—The Sa-
voy Grill. What did you have?—The *rognons de veau* was superb.—
And claret?— Yes, a great glass of claret." . . . I like that, because
there's so much bullshit about preparing for your part. These were
actors who just knew that when you got on the stage, you acted.
When it started, and not before.

HAROLD PINTER, observing John Gielgud and Ralph Richardson
in his play *No Man's Land*

contents

ACT I

Towards
the End of
the Day

Fade in on a painted theatre curtain, dirty, worn and ragged. Silence. No music. Then knocks and banging can be heard in the wings.

I begin with what is called a "stage direction," in which the theatre itself seems to be the play. But it also feels like indications from a film script; it's on screen that images fade in and out, as slippery as transformation or instability. On stage, appearance is a steadier, dogged presence, appealing at first, but soon helpless or static. Unless the sense of place and décor is elastic, soaring, and in the mind. But saying that leads us to theory and the argument of this extended essay:

For whereas we feel a first thrill when the opening curtain reveals a staged place, or when "reality" dawns on a screen, still we can hardly embark on a study of acting without acknowledging that its attempt at realism or actuality is forlorn and self-defeating. Acting is an escape from reality, as well as an exultation or despair over it. I warn you that the more strenuously real a play or a movie claims to be, the quicker I become bored. The only honorable reality is that of pretending, but that is sufficient reason why acting matters beyond all differences in style, pay grade, or how "good" the process is.

We like to propose that some acting is better than others: so Brando, Olivier, or Day-Lewis (recurring figures in this book) are superior to your Uncle Arthur, the Christmas bore when he does his bits of Shakespeare, or vaudeville. But the same connoisseur cavils over the masters: so Olivier was too cold, Brando gave up his calling, and Day-Lewis gets lost in his roles. Sometimes he was Hamlet for days at a time until he suffered the prince's breakdown. But Arthur labors on with his art and his life year after year without pay or reviews. He may know he is not very "good" or convincing; that hardly matters; no one does his part the way he does it.

We might as well start by admitting that all acting is "bad" as much as it is "good": it could be improved; it is immoral and distracting in that it puts the humbug of ultimate Truth above tedious daily honesty, or the attempt at it; and it is dangerous in that it allows us to give up on "to thine own self be true," while trying to be anyone and everyone. Acting is so essential or inescapable that it easily absorbs and welcomes bad acting. So let us toss out that old chestnut that the play or the actor may help us "to live better." There is no help. The purpose of acting is to evade such considerations—and you can see how fruitful it has been.

The enthusiasm for acting that has intensified in the past five hundred years, or two thousand, whichever size blink you prefer, has come about because we have been drawn to pretense or avoidance beyond any hope for reality. As a rule, we make a mess of reality, whether it is our own and Uncle Arthur's lives or the Fate of the Earth. As it becomes clearer that the evolution of weather may overwhelm us, drown us, dry us out like bones in the desert, so we love the fertile fictional places more and more—Shakespeare's Arden, Beckett's desolate country road, John Ford's Monument Valley, or the Paris of the French New

Wave. Acting and the space in which acting occurs matter because they are the material of a ritual to be beheld while we give up our ghost. This evasion or experiment can exist on stage or screen, at the opera, at the ballet, or at a soccer match where a player tries to be himself, or even when a tipsy Uncle Arthur strives to say what life is about. Only the passage of time has to be filled, and when we are fearful of our time being suddenly stopped, we love the dream that we can control it by taking creative charge and replacing uncertainty with performance.

Yet there are other things that "matter" so fundamentally that it seems folly to brood on them—Why breathing matters? Or taking nourishment, falling asleep, or waking? Such urges have been there since our beginning—haven't they? We seem to be helpless in those processes, or beyond responsibility. So why ask the question about them? Even without much "scientific" knowledge in those areas, I can see that breathing and feeding are instincts, like putting one foot ahead of another in the process of walking. But even in my ignorance, I think I can see how the question "Why does waking up matter?" reaches beyond instinct into consciousness and desire. There does not have to be a God, or a god anywhere. Still, after a busy day of fear, hunger, solitude, and raw nothingness—all in the most perfect jungle or desert—if something in a being hopes to wake up tomorrow and try it all again, then at least there is some thought of improvement, of yearning, some way in which the place and the air have moved us. Here is the start of religion and philosophy, of art and "the future." It's like using italic type. Why am I saying the place seems "perfect," or so much more arranged and calm than my life? Is there something called "beauty"? Why would beauty matter? Is it a natural state of creation or evolution? Is there anywhere natural on earth that is not beautiful? Or is that faith simply my urge to see and exist in something to be known as beauty?

The thing depicted in acting may be hideous and profoundly upsetting. It may be Gloucester having his eyes put out in *Lear*, or Sophie presented with her choice in William Styron's novel and the film that was made of it.[1] Those are such terrible moments that it may feel indecent to make an act or a pretending out of them. But we persist and we ask "beauty" to come to the merciful aid of existence in the process.

I am going to say something now that is upsetting. It may offend you. But sometimes the cause of creative offense matters. So consider the situation in *Sophie's Choice*. That trembling, pale mother, Meryl Streep,* is presented with the chance of saving one child and condemning another. We are "in" a concentration camp—her cruel choice is as much a prison for our mind and

*Of course, Meryl Streep is not the mother (though she does have children); yet she is the mother. She has to be. In other words, we have lived through the age in which actors "represented" their parts, and we have arrived at a time when we take pleasure in watching the role and the player wrestle together—sometimes in movies it is as erotic as "lovemaking." So I am talking about Sophie here, and perhaps I should say that. But it is Streep, too, and even in 1982, which was early in her astonishing career, we took pleasure in obeying the command of the film—see Streep do Sophie, with accent, look, and aura. Professional protocol, and copyediting, may say, "Don't confuse the two." But the fun and the madness in pretending says, "Do what you must." There is a further point in this case: it may be more comfortable, or bearable, to watch Streep playing (or singing) than to think of Sophie being there.

being as it is for her. Yet we are watching, too, like someone in a laboratory or a theatre observing an attempt to describe life more closely.

We know what Styron and Streep did. But let me add an improv: Sophie tells the Nazi, "I can't decide. You make the choice. Toss a coin." The officer immediately loses a layer of his revolting authority. He pats his pockets. He says, "I don't have a coin. Nazis don't carry money." At which point, the story slips into a demented search for a coin in the camp. For neither the prisoners nor the guards have currency. Here is the shock: the situation begins to be comic; it turns towards screwball; and lo and behold, the Nazi and Sophie start to become like Cary Grant and Katharine Hepburn looking for a leopard in the forests of Connecticut.

That remake is hideous, you say, and appalling—so, if nothing else, you have rediscovered a way to be shocked by a brand of action that has often become a cliché in seventy years—I mean what happened in the camps. You may burst out, "Oh, you can't do such things!" But I can, if I have daring enough and talent to pull it off, and if I can find a fresh form for the horror. The miracle of pretending is that we have learned in a few hundred years that anything may work. So, in fact, we do sit still for the murderousness of Michael Corleone, and for the removal of Gloucester's eyes (six nights a week, with a Wednesday matinee). Perhaps our best retaliation to such numbing terror—our innate urge to wake up—is to make a play of such things that says, yes, there is still a chance of beauty or hope, or playfulness. Perhaps acting matters because of our dying attempt to believe that life is not simply a desperate terrifying process in which we are alone and insignificant. Acting may matter because we resist that atrocious plan.

But if a book implies a question in its title, then the child in us anticipates an answer. And we like to fall into the faux wisdom that says, "Of course, we are a species that asks impossible questions—aren't we?"

Now, there is history in this essay, without its turning into a history book. It has to be said that whereas breathing, eating, and sleeping go back as far as our species, we are uncertain about when "acting" began. I will make a few modest or playful suggestions about that, while noting that we know the names of actors only from the late sixteenth century onwards. Not that we know how good Richard Burbage was . . . or Edmund Kean, or even Henry Irving. Were they better than the great Joseph Tura?[2] One day, Daniel Day-Lewis may be no more urgent than a name on the wall written in old script. Even so, acting has surely come to matter much more in the past hundred years as media arrived that could make it available for everyone. And more or less, in that new age most of us have looked at acting. We have been thrilled and amused, and we have taken actors and actresses into our private imaginary worlds.

We have even thought that we wouldn't mind being like that—or if barred from the thing itself, by looks, elocution, or talent, well, we could pretend to be actors (or audience).

■

Hurrah! We're going to the show, and we're as excited as the Cratchit family on Christmas morning with an epic turkey roasting in the oven! So let us be quite clear—turn to some other book if you do not share in an uncritical love for actors; we revere them, we need them. They nourish us; they entertain us. We have been changed by them (not that this made any useful difference). They are so gorgeous—and *casual.* How can they be so immaculate and nonchalant at the same time—Are they saying lines? Or are they possessed by some natural grace? So much of hope, dream, and desire rests with them. Don't we go to actors as we might seek analysts or witch doctors or forgiving lovers, on the chance of being made whole? I know, we are respectable and pompous now—we tell ourselves we are going to see this important new play, or the movie that is the talk of the intelligent classes, those lofty works. But it's the pretending that gets us, theirs and ours. If they can be extraordinary for an hour, we may dream of a new life. They act and we are acted on. It is the bargain of our history.

Reality is no longer what it was—or what it ought to be. People sat in packed theatres to watch movies during a war when bombing raids might have lowered the roof! When Laurence Olivier made *Henry V* at the close of that war, he turned seeing Shakespeare into a patriotic duty.

That is not rhetoric. With *Henry V, Hamlet,* and *Richard III,* Olivier helped shape a modern industry of Shakespeare as a tourist commodity and a source of pride. This taste was begun by Lillian Bayliss at the Old Vic theatre in 1912, the Royal Shakespeare Company (an offshoot of the annual festival at Stratford-on-Avon), and then the National Theatre itself. As Britain gave up on producing automobiles, battleships, and stiff upper lips

(Olivier had a mouth like a straight edge), so it found Shakespeare and theatre, scandals and sensual lower lips—as witness Mick Jagger, Timothy Spall, and Rebecca Hall. That midcentury urge for Shakespeare was also spurred on by the collective of remarkable new actors available—Olivier, Gielgud, Ralph Richardson, Michael Redgrave, Alec Guinness, all born within the years 1902–14.

One of the sharpest moments in the movie of *Henry V* is at the start, in the glimpse of an unknown Elizabethan actor in the wings, hushed, nervous, in awe of his own occasion, waiting to step on to the glowing stage of the Globe to be the King. Of course, Olivier played both parts in his film, the common man and the transforming example. No one loved acting more than he did, or had such expectations for being changed.

The show! It comes in many forms—a play done on a stage; a movie thrown up on a screen; or even some feverish melodrama on television, jammed between the sofa and that absurd potted rubber tree—though television is not humble any more: it believes it deserves to be a sleek black plasma oblong hanging on the wall, with a remote that is complicated enough to launch a nuclear attack. But we should add dancers in a ballet; singers in an opera; and don't leave out the players and the conductor in an orchestra. After all, that band of brothers and sisters could come to us on the radio, as a CD—and authorities argue that the sound then is clearer or more emphatic. But some of us like to go to the concert hall, to see them all acting like musicians. I don't mean to suggest they are *not* musicians (though I suppose today they might be miming). But we like to see them play the part. Come to that, I may think tomorrow afternoon of going to see Real Madrid versus Barcelona to see how well Lionel Messi and Cristiano Ronaldo manage to be themselves (as opposed to lackluster, off-day stand-ins, not quite the real thing).

Those players will be there, earning their money. Messi will look deferential, insignificant, and even furtive—until he strikes —while Ronaldo, no matter how he plays, will have a matador swagger and those overdone, or old-fashioned, movie-star looks. His income is entirely modern, but he looks like a silent star. It may only be in pulling up a sock, or waving a hand of fatalistic, forgiving disbelief when a pass fails to reach him, but for a moment or two he will be "Ronaldo," someone we have come to see. At Manchester United and Real Madrid, there are kids —like the Cratchits—who watched him for the first time with the wonder that Tiny Tim felt when he sniffed the turkey drippings. That's why Cristiano Ronaldo dos Santos Aveiro (born in Funchal, Madeira, and named Ronaldo after Ronald Reagan, his father's favorite actor) gets €21 million a year—because enough of us have hurrah in our hearts when he moves. In a Spanish La Liga season, he makes about thirty-five appearances, with another twenty games in cup competitions and the Champions League. In 2012–13, he played fifty-five times and scored fifty-five goals. He earns another $21 million a year on sponsorship deals with Armani, Nike, Castrol, and many other companies. In early 2014, he won the Copa de Oro—for the best player, best of the best. If he announced he would do *Hamlet,* it would be a sell-out. Why bother? In three or four games a season he *is* Hamlet, magnificent yet undone by fate, hardly knowing whether to be or not, or flash that cheeky "Ronaldo" smile round the stadium, like a blessing. Didn't Ronald Reagan have that same all-purpose, smothering grin as if to say, "What do you expect, guys—I *am* the president. Look in the program."

Ronaldo reminds one of Valentino or Tyrone Power, as well as being the contemporary soccer player with perhaps the sharpest sense of show business. (He's Carol Burnett doing Tyrone Power. He's gorgeous, indecently skilled, but fatuous.) You may say that his play, his athleticism, are natural. But you cannot watch him (and struggle with feelings of awe and disdain) without recognizing that he is camp. Win or lose, in triumph or chagrin, he is *like* "Ronaldo."

When did this gesture towards resemblance (unique but infinite) come into being? It can't always have been there, though it is possible that cavemen began to paint their lives on cave walls to exult and to manage their fears and their loneliness. That first appreciation of irony must have been a turning point, but maybe it took centuries. It was 1945 before anyone thought to add that hesitant figure of the actor about to be King to *Henry V.*

But the idea of acting is increasingly active in our culture, and decreasingly the property of professionals. In 1961 Walker Percy published a novel, *The Moviegoer,* that had uncanny insight into how mundane an acting star could be. The book is set in New Orleans and the central character is Binx Bolling, a lost soul, a man who goes to the movies a lot for their special moments and for the sheltering light they cast on his unhappy life. Early in the story, Percy does a conjuring trick. Binx gets off a bus in the city center, and watches the passersby. Who should come out of an alley ahead but William Holden?! But it's Holden without a role, a script, or a movie. All he has are his performing airs or habits.

We never know whether this is a ghost, a dream, a literary conceit, a real holden, or the actual Holden. But the resemblance is everything: "He is an attractive fellow with his ordinary good looks, very sun-tanned, walking along hands in pockets, raincoat slung over one shoulder."

If you've ever seen William Holden, then you know this figure —you know him as Joe Gillis from *Sunset Blvd,* and in 1960 you might have seen him lately in *Sabrina, Picnic, The Bridge on the River Kwai,* and so on. Very few reckoned him a great actor: he could hardly have played, or wanted to play, Iago to Olivier's Othello. But in his own territory he was reliable, bankable, a gift to so many films, known and liked by the public, and always reminiscent of "William Holden." He had an ease on screen, an absent presence that Olivier would never trust.

In *The Moviegoer,* he strolls along and a young couple on a rather awkward honeymoon recognize him. "Holden slaps his pockets for a match"—we know that gesture. The boy offers him a light. Holden takes it. They exchange a few words. The honeymoon is enhanced and vindicated. And the ghost moves on:

Holden has turned down Toulouse shedding light as he goes. An aura of heightened reality moves with him and all who fall within it feel it.

This Holden never reappears in the novel. He was only there as a screened figure, though it tells us important things about Binx that he is impressed by the "peculiar reality" Holden gives off. Just as the boy on honeymoon has become a man of the world in providing a light, so Binx's solitude has been fixed. William Holden played many parts, and some of them ended as badly as Joe Gillis. But he had a suntanned ordinariness that had the grace to be photographed without ever noticing the theft or intrusion. He was an actor, and as pleasing as an open window we could walk through.

He still is. Actors conduct many experiments on our behalf, not the least of which is that for more than a hundred years they have been trying out eternal life. Let me explain.

William Holden (or William Franklin Beedle—Bill Beedle, I daresay) died in November 1981, and it was not what we think of as a good death. He was sixty-three then, far from old, yet people reckoned he looked older than his age. He had been a hard drinker for decades, and that suntanned, lined face had turned grim. In *Network*—where he is as satisfying as he ever was—he was only fifty-eight yet he was depicted as a world-weary veteran of television. In November 1981 he was alone in his apartment in Santa Monica. Divorced from his wife, Brenda Marshall (an actress), he had had relationships with two other actresses, Capucine and Stefanie Powers, but liquor had stood in the way of attachment. He was probably not a happy man, and certainly not as relaxed as he was paid to be on screen. He had been drinking in his apartment that day. He seems to have slipped on a rug. As he fell, he cut open his head on a piece of solid furniture, and he bled to death. The body was not discovered for four days.[3]

There are worse deaths. A little more than two years before the discovery of Holden, policemen in Paris noticed a car endlessly parked on the rue de General Appert. And so, on September 8, 1979, at the end of summer, they opened the unlocked door and a hideous stench came out. It marked the body of the actress Jean Seberg, curled up in a blanket and already decomposing after ten days. She had killed herself and no one had noticed. But about twenty years earlier she had been the last girl left in an international search for someone to play Saint Joan. In Paris, she had written a note for her young son: "Forgive me. I can no longer live with my nerves."[4]

Holden's body was cremated and the ashes were scattered in the Pacific. He had asked that there be no memorial service. So it's easy to say he closed the door on himself. But then as people had not managed before his time, he remained alive—not as a registered being; he had no vote, no taxes to pay, and no wardrobe to mull over—but in the capacity that may have meant the most to him: as an actor and an icon, patting his pockets for a match and then strolling down the street, passing a word here or there. Jean Seberg is still the kid on the street selling the *New York Herald Tribune* in *Breathless;* it's the newspaper that has passed. People had been acquiring a new grip on perpetuity since the 1830s: exact photographic images exist from that time. Sixty or so years later, those images moved. Another thirty years and they spoke, chuckled, or sighed. I daresay even now you can conjure up Bill Holden's light, friendly but faintly sour voice, like that of a man who never much believed in himself.

He's still here. You can enjoy the disbelief on Joe Gillis's face as he begins to realize the demented nature of Norma Desmond's existence. You can see Holden leaving that house on Sunset, and toppling into the pool as Norma shoots him. Most remarkable of all, there is that view from the bottom of the pool, looking up at the spread-eagled Joe staring down, dead, but still a rippling image and starting to tell us the story of *Sunset Blvd.* You could say that his most enduring moment is that instant of death, and that shot is sixty-three years old now (his age when he hit his head).

I wonder whether writer-director Billy Wilder would have thought to employ this device if he had not had fifty years or so of seeing that actors aged and died while their image stayed young?

You can see Holden's Pike in *The Wild Bunch,* feeling the pain in his leg as he mounts a horse, and saying, "Let's do it," to the last of the bunch, before they walk into their magnificent and appointed deaths in the battle with Mapache and his ragtag army. You can see Holden staggering out of the river in *The Bridge on the River Kwai,* determined to press the fatal plunger. You can see him with Kim Novak in that mauve-lilac dress in *Picnic,* dancing with her to "Moonglow." I don't know that there was anything between them—except that magical scene. You can even see that preserved moment at the Academy Awards of 1978 where he interrupts proceedings to tell Barbara Stanwyck and the world what a champ she had been—and she was the female lead in Holden's first important picture, *Golden Boy.* He had been golden once—just look at his blond hair and his boyish smile in *I Wanted Wings* or *Blaze of Noon.*

I am not picking on Holden because he is one of our greatest actors. It's more that—as Walker Percy recognized—he had a kind of empty splendor that just waited to be on film and which was as obedient as all actors have to be, waiting to be cast. There are a few thousand actors who still "live" on film, though not so many who have such a body of work as Holden. For instance, with seventy-seven films, he has a bank of imagery so that anyone so inclined could feed his digitized appearance into a computer and generate fairly convincing new movie footage of William Holden. I'm not saying they should, but the possibility is there and it testifies that Holden is current still. Time passes and young people forget. A day will come when as few people recollect him as they do Robert Harron and Miriam Cooper now (they were actors with D. W. Griffith). But so long as archives endure and the imagery can be preserved, Holden will be alive or in that movie life that meant so much to him. I don't mean to be facetious or sacrilegious, but he has the beginning of eternal life (which is more than Burbage or Kean possesses).

There are other figures from modern history in that same category—Churchill, Hitler, Kennedy—and I feel that they began to act up under the spur of the camera: imagine Hitler watching *Triumph of the Will* and taking notes on his own presentation. There is newsreel of Mussolini where he nods in affirmation at a roar of applause as if to say, "I nailed that!" But with those world-stage tycoons (movie fans, all of them) we do not have the moments of idleness that Holden offered, the close-ups where he thinks to himself, the private wry grins that went to millions, the inwardness of plain Bill Holden. His nature? His soul? It's an experiment still as to what word we settle on, but in human history this was a new condition that came with sound-on-film, and it's not going too far to call it life after death.

It doesn't "save" Holden in any spiritual sense. It can't bring him comfort. But it does something to us, I think, and adds to the high esteem we have for the adventure of acting. It's one thing to save South Africa from apartheid or discover the Higgs boson. But it's another to have your smile hanging in the air as a universal sign of ease.

◾

Was William Holden "better than" Edmund Kean (1787–1833)?[5] Would Jack Johnson have defeated Muhammad Ali? We'll never know, not just because of the limits of recording technology, but because we act upon the assumption (I did say "act") that you had to be there to know. What that means is that you had to see Kean in London or in America, from 1814 onwards, in the years of his glory and daring. He had been born in Westminster, the child of a clerk and an actress, people of few means. But he showed promise as an actor as a child, and he was taught by an uncle, Moses Kean, in mime and energetic enactment. Edmund was small of stature but brimming with inner urgings.

Of course, he didn't burst, but "bursting with inner demons" is the kind of story we tell about actors when there is hardly any record of them. In just a few adult years Kean became a sensation in London doing Shylock, Richard III, Hamlet, Othello, Macbeth, Lear. Would it have been possible for a great actor then to be identified without the existence of Shakespeare? By which, I mean we have to consider that one dramatist introduced the prospect and potential of acting beyond any other playwright because the nature of being and acting was itself *the* Shakespearean subject.

Invariably when a new acting wonder comes on the scene, like a beacon, he is said to have revealed unprecedented realism or naturalism. Shakespeare's gravity was often muffled in Kean's day. More than a hundred years earlier, Nahum Tate had rewritten *Lear* so that it had a happy ending, in which Cordelia survived (and married Edgar). The Fool had been cut out! By instinct or rebellion, Kean knew that genteel salvation was humbug and damaging. So he went back to Shakespeare's text and came on stage with his dead daughter in his arms. Audiences were deeply moved, and they have been ever since, even if some Lears have wished their Cordelia was a little lighter. It was said that Byron fainted in a theatre while watching Kean. Coleridge the poet claimed that beholding Kean was "like reading Shakespeare by flashes of lightning."[6] (What does that signify, apart from the poet's urge to show that something new and thrilling had happened *to him?* A hundred years later, President Woodrow Wilson would say that *The Birth of a Nation* was like history written with lightning. Or Griffith's publicists said he had said that.)[7]

Kean himself reported that he "could not feel the stage under him." He was floating; he was high. Audiences were aroused and stricken, but in the end they resisted his heady "realism" and called for the return of the Tate version. Kean yielded and so Cordelia rose from the dead.

He did not live long, and at the end, when he was playing Othello with his son as Iago, he broke out of the text and lunged further towards naturalism by crying out, "I am dying." He was known for turbulence and eccentricity. Sometimes he seemed to believe he had been taken over by a part. Did he really keep a lion as a pet? Did he seduce all those women? Would he have been—in our eyes—a toxic celebrity and tiresome overactor? Does that matter? As it is, he is one of a handful of names that trace the history of acting from Thespis to Burbage, to Garrick and beyond. His was the sword, wasn't it?

The story goes that in 1930, a dealer in memorabilia appeared at the dressing room of John Gielgud, who had just played Hamlet at the Old Vic. "Mr. Gielgud," he says, "I have the very sword that was Edmund Kean's, and I believe you are now its rightful owner." Gielgud was taken aback but he accepted. It was said that the sword had come down by way of Henry Irving, but no one knows.[8] Then as time went by, in another fifteen years or so, Gielgud presented the sword to Laurence Olivier. Olivier was moved with gratitude and he kept the blade. Near his death, his third wife (all actresses), Joan Plowright, wondered what he was going to do with it. Could he not offer it to a younger and deserving actor? Olivier hesitated, but never passed it on.

Was it really Kean's sword? That is like trying to determine whether one piece of lead was the real Maltese Falcon, or one wooden plank the Rosebud sled. The culture of acting needs the sword—we may remember that the figure of Oscar holds a sword. There are paintings of Kean, popular images, but no photograph. We have enough to suggest he was small, dark and intense and possibly Jewish. In many of the pictures he looks like someone trying to assert the fact that he is an actor. You can tell from his expression that any actor fights a battle of belief—with the audience and with himself. One of the first English people to write searchingly about acting was William Hazlitt, who said of Kean's Richard III: "In the rapidity of his transitions from one tone and feeling to another, in propriety and novelty of action, presenting a succession of striking pictures and giving perpetually fresh shocks of delight and surprise, it would be difficult to single out a competitor."[9]

Only three years after Kean's death, Alexandre Dumas wrote a play about the bright shocker, *Kean: A Play in V Acts,* that reveled in the contrasts in Kean's life—received by royalty, acclaimed by society, but living in the underworld—drink, drugs, women, you know this pattern. The play was a success, and the title role was taken by Frédérick Lemaître, the actor depicted in Marcel Carne's film *Les Enfants du Paradis.* In that 1944 movie, Lemaître exults, "When I act, I am desperately in love. . . . But when the curtain falls, the audience goes away and takes 'my love' with it."[10] So make sure the play never stops!

By 1954 Jean-Paul Sartre had been so inspired that he took the Dumas text and adapted it into a new play, *Kean,* in which the adventures of the actor are material for a wry, philosophical examination of acting, naturalism, and fraud. It is a play of brilliant language and existential riddles. In its first production, Kean was played by Pierre Brasseur, the actor who had played Lemaître in *Les Enfants du Paradis.* There are moments in the play when Kean talks of himself as a pretender with no soul of his own—though it is not clear whether he laments this or glories in it:

> We believe that men need illusion—that one can live and die for something other than cheese. What have you done? You took a child, and you turned him into an actor—an illusion, a fantasy—

that is what you have made of Kean. He is sham prince, sham miser, sham general, sham king. Apart from that nothing. He is a national treasure. But on condition that he makes no attempt to live a real life. In an hour from now, I shall take an old whore in my arms, and all London will cry "Vivat!" But if I kiss the hands of a woman I love, I shall find myself torn in pieces. Do you understand that I want to weigh with my real weight in the world? That I have had enough of being a shadow in a magic lantern? For twenty years I have been acting a part to amuse you all. Can't you understand that I want to live my own life?[11]

From Kean to Lindsay Lohan, nearly every player has felt that pang, and some of them have guessed that even the sincere outburst felt like a speech written for them. It was shortly after Kean's death, by chance, that Denis Diderot's *Paradoxe sur le Comedien* was published in France. Written nearly fifty years earlier, this book dwells on a Kean-like riddle: how can the actor so move other people, except by being coldblooded himself? It was the origin of a notion whereby the fake might be a shaman.

Kean is a play that appeals to willful actors, and subsequently the role has been taken on by Vittorio Gassman, Alfred Drake (in a musical version), Alan Badel, Anthony Sher, Jean-Paul Belmondo, Anthony Hopkins, and Ben Kingsley. So Kean as a spokesman for disordered brilliance endures. But the historic Kean was a player of whom we know nothing, except that crowds noticed him.

■

No situation is more clinching in the question of how acting matters than when and how one is impressed by a particular show. It doesn't have to be a great play. I am talking about being gripped for the first time by the intimacy of performance. It is as if the show has been arranged for you, as if it knew your secret being. *The Entertainer,* it seems to me now, is not as novel or searching as *Look Back in Anger,* its predecessor. But *The Entertainer* was written under special circumstances. In the first place, Laurence Olivier had challenged John Osborne to write it for him. In response, Osborne retaliated as if to say, "Well, see if you dare play this."

Look Back in Anger opened at the Royal Court Theatre in London in the spring of 1956. It was a play about young people, and especially about Jimmy Porter, railing against the boredom and hypocrisy of his Britain. Tony Richardson directed, and the cast included Kenneth Haigh (as Porter) and Mary Ure (as Jimmy's wife). The play was widely attacked by London critics, but the two most important—Harold Hobson and Kenneth Tynan—rallied to it. Tynan went so far as to say he could not love anyone who didn't love *Look Back in Anger.*[12]

Critics, or reviewers, have to say something, and invariably they have been moved by proximity to the drama. They need to feel it's about them. Tynan had acted himself as a younger man; he had something of an act all his life. Critics want to be a part of the play, so they come close to dramatizing themselves. His biography suggests that Tynan was not always so discriminating in choosing those he loved.

One night, Laurence Olivier and Arthur Miller went together to see *Look Back in Anger.* Miller was in England with his wife, Marilyn Monroe, as she acted opposite Olivier in the movie *The Sleeping Prince.* Olivier was directing, too, and the shooting was going slowly and reluctantly. At the theatre, Olivier warned the American playwright not to expect too much. But Miller was excited by *Look Back in Anger.* He "loved the play's roughness and self-indulgences, its flinging high in the air so many pomposities of Britishism, its unbridled irritation with life, and its verbal energy."[13] He was reminded of the young Clifford Odets, and he probably felt an energy breaking out of an England where he was uneasy. Olivier was intimidated—actors are seldom confident judges of material. After the show, they met Osborne, and on impulse Olivier said, "Perhaps you could write something for me." This was the greatest actor of his nation and his time asking a new playwright for a part because Olivier had been taken aback by Miller's reaction to the play.

The result was *The Entertainer,* which viewed Britain during the 1956 Suez crisis through the eyes of the family of Archie Rice, a third-rate music-hall comedian. The play was a commentary on the loss of imperial confidence, matched by the decline of music hall (under the pressure of television). The play opened at the Royal Court in the spring of 1957. So I was sixteen when I saw it, from the front row of the balcony. In my memory, I seemed to be jutting out into the darkness, where the actors were little more than fifteen feet away—make an allowance, say it was twenty-five. I had not seen Olivier live before; I had seen only a few plays; but in advance my parents had told me that I was going to see Britain's great actor—so I was prepared for grandeur or quality and the arresting way in which he was "solus."

John Osborne had taken this into account. If Olivier had been slumming a little in seeking to get involved with the Royal

Court, Osborne would rub his nose in it. Archie is a cheat and a failure—he cheats on his wife, his family, and his income tax, and he despises his audience, which is the worst betrayal in an actor. Moreover, the play was done with regular scenes of family life, and then with Archie on stage at the nudie review for which he was the comic. He wore a bowler hat, a loud check jacket, a bow tie like a dildo, a cane, and a rictus grin. He was odious, slimy, pathetic, and the lowest life Olivier had ever chosen to play. But he was an arresting, insolent scoundrel, dishonesty made supreme. Those few feet away I could see the greasepaint on his face and imagine the decay. The theatre often smells, and sometimes it is makeup in the heat of the lights, and the sweat-soaked costumes.

It wasn't that I asked myself whether Olivier was accurate, or credible, or "good" as Archie Rice. I never considered whether the play had merit. But I was taken with the proximity and pulse of someone pretending for me, and I know that I felt that because the structure of *The Entertainer* asked us to see Archie stepping away from family failure into his brief, gaudy spotlight. It was a play about acting, and I was entertained in the full sense of that odd word.

Is entertainment a matter of having time passed, or filled? *The word* comes large and small. The dictionary starts by saying it is simply amusement or diversion, but then it owns up to "admitting something into the mind." That something could be the laws of relativity or Robert Musil's *The Man Without Qualities*. It could be an enormous adventure, as in *Henry V* when the Chorus asks us to "entertain conjecture of a time." How grand and resonant that is. Yet it's no more than "let's pretend." With this proviso: that if we are asked to pretend, there can be no question of an ultimate and reliable reality. So in the film of *Henry V* we shift from the wooden Globe and its Giotto-like sets to the lush green meadows of Wicklow in Ireland. But still we can't walk on the grass or smell the dung as the horses trot by.

How was a lousy comic like Archie Rice so riveting? Years later, I found a book where Orson Welles talked about Olivier's Archie. Welles is a curious figure in this context. He had one or two extraordinary performances (Kane is the greatest), but all too often he was a hammy actor, underprepared or unduly contemptuous of the rubbish he was doing. Still, as an observer of actors he was often piercing:

> You see, Larry can't bear to fail, even if he's supposed to fail. So when he played the comic onstage, he played for real laughs from the paying audience, instead of giving the feeling that he was in a half-empty theatre where nobody was laughing. He did not play a failed comedian. Success to Larry demanded being an effective comedian, even though it made no sense![14]

I never felt that when I was sixteen; yet looking back, I think Welles was correct. The slug in Archie had become a bright lizard, an iguana, or a snake, and I felt like a rabbit, unable to escape his gaze. Olivier's Archie knew he was a standup ghost for the decline of everything, in just the way Shakespeare's Gloucester is so mercilessly eloquent about "the winter of our discontent." In 1957 there were two figures of death in acting: one wore a dark shroud in Bergman's *The Seventh Seal,* and the other was Olivier's garish Archie, an alarming barker for the graveyard.

Equally, one might have rebuked Welles by saying that his own Charles Foster Kane was just a commonplace American millionaire failure—but it was Welles who refused to make him other than riveting and seductive.

I never cared about *The Entertainer* as a play, but I had never felt an actor be so compelling. Of course, I knew Archie was "a part," and I did not realize that Olivier had seldom played a role that was not royalty, or gripped by ambition. He admits in a memoir that he was most vexed when Ralph Richardson was knighted before he was. That was all part of what Welles saw as Olivier's lust for success and status. I was by instinct wary of stage acting—I had fallen in love with the immaculate fantasy of film. But I was riveted by the idea of a real person pretending to do this, and I had seen enough pictures of Olivier (including *Henry V*) to know that Archie was a serious reach, although Olivier's appearance could be mercurial, or even shifty. He did not often look like himself. But Archie was uncanny pretending, and I could not take my eyes off it. I remember little else about the evening, which included Brenda De Banzie, George Relph, and Dorothy Tutin (who was having a quiet affair with Olivier, but would be replaced by Joan Plowright when the production moved on to the West End—and one day Olivier would marry Plowright, after his troubled marriage to Vivien Leigh had ended).

Olivier's Archie Rice mattered, to me. I could feel something I wasn't able to articulate: that this glittering wreck only a few feet away was as vital as one's father in life, drunk or sober. And that attachment has formed at other times for me in theatrical situations: with Patrick McGoohan in Ibsen's *Brand;* watching Ian Bannen in *Serjeant Musgrave's Dance,* or Faith and Lyndon Brook in *The Kidders,* by Donald Ogden Stewart; with Patrick Magee in *Krapp's Last Tape,* with Lena Horne in a live show in London, and Stan Getz in Oakland; with Maggie Smith in *The Country Wife,* with Alan Badel as *Kean,* with Daniel Day-Lewis in a yellow coat in a play called *The Futurists;* with everyone in the New York production of *Into the Woods,* and a few others, including Jerry Lewis trying to drink a rogue glass of water on stage in San Francisco.

I fell in love with people on the screen all the time. But that felt less possible or polite on stage. Actual presence often had the effect of restricting my imagination. But Archie Rice taught me so much about the space called theatre, the terrible exposure of being a comedian, to say nothing of the intricacies of being Laurence Olivier. There was some way in which the role had freed the rascal in him, and he luxuriated in it, like Salome between the fourth and fifth veils.

The shock value of Olivier as Archie Rice in 1957 owed something to the unlikelihood of casting. In his own mind and in public regard, he was so much a gentleman, even a bloodied nobleman. He had played Hamlet and Lear and Macbeth; he had been Maxim de Winter in *Rebecca* and a Heathcliff in the American *Wuthering Heights* who was more lord of the house than urchin; he had been Mr. Darcy, Astrov, Lord Nelson, and Oedipus. It was his habit to be handsome and well spoken. He had died on stage and film, of course; he was already famous for his dying falls, but they were inspirational and aristocratic (like his noses). He could claim one spectacular villain, Richard III (based, as he said, on his memories of the hateful American director Jed Harris), but Richard was a king and a peerless monster, rhapsodic in the malice of his own soliloquy. There was nothing humble or downcast about him. On stage and screen still the overall English tendency was to celebrate the upper, educated, or refined classes. The Kowalskis in *A Streetcar Named Desire* are working class. In *Death of a Salesman* especially, Arthur Miller wanted to defy that stagy class system by taking a protagonist who is an ostensible failure and to "win out over anonymity and meaninglessness, to love and be loved, and above all perhaps, to *count*."[15] I don't think Olivier had ever played or contemplated playing a character threatened by meaninglessness.

He had been knighted in 1947 at the age of forty, after his blond *Hamlet* had won Best Picture. The marriage to Vivien Leigh was still looked at by the public as something made in heaven.[16] And yet, I suspect John Osborne had seen something duplicitous in Olivier, or felt the actor's need to come clean. The whole question of how far it is proper to go into an actor's private life is upon us—despite the Kean-like complaint about having no privacy.

The business of entertainment cannot look away from the marketable celebrity of actors. Before movies, leading actors were seen by only a fraction of the public. The screen ended that isolation, and it offered the actors in a way theatre had never possessed: it did them in close-up so that they were obliged to be better looking. Olivier could say he had worked his way up gradually by dint of hard work. But Vivien Leigh had been struck by magic. She was the victor in the immense search for Scarlett O'Hara, a process that had had more to do with public relations than the accuracy of casting. She became a marvel in a year.

Olivier and Leigh were romantic celebrities, in a postwar Britain short on glamour or stars; so they were duty-bound to provide something. They had been famous lovers, giving up earlier marriages and children to be together. In fact, they were soon both inclined to look elsewhere for sexual adventure. Much more dangerous, Vivien Leigh was unbalanced.

She also threatened Olivier. He was older than she was and farther on in his career. But just as he went to Goldwyn to make *Wuthering Heights,* so Vivien rather sneaked up on him, came to America without his knowing, secured the most treasured role of Scarlett O'Hara, carried that film to its glory, and won the Oscar. In contrast, Olivier felt he had never quite proved himself as a movie star. Years earlier, Garbo and the director Rouben Mamoulian had decided that Olivier didn't have enough excitement on screen to play with her in *Queen Christina.*[17] He was callow next to her. Not sexy enough for Garbo—that's a tombstone line, and a spine of insecurity. His Heathcliff in *Wuthering Heights* was fine, but it lacked smiles and glamour. Most people in the business felt Olivier was a more accomplished actor than Leigh— or more intelligent, more versatile and controlled. But he was not convinced he could carry a big picture, and as anyone who knew him understood, he was a demon of competition. He got his acting Oscar in *Hamlet* (1948); the film was an artistic success and a box office coup in America. But then Leigh won a second Oscar as Blanche DuBois in *A Streetcar Named Desire.* Born in India and raised in South Kensington, she relied less on the kindness of strangers than on southern belles, one selfish, the other cracked.

The Tennessee Williams play had opened on Broadway in December 1947 as a sensation. That was because of its poetic sexuality; because of the intense psychological exploration made by its director, Elia Kazan; and because of Marlon Brando's Stanley Kowalski—a rough, working-class brute, but as helplessly beautiful as Brando. Kazan was also a founding member of the Actors Studio and instrumental in the application of Russian naturalism and sense memory as outlined by Konstantin Stanislavsky and about to be enshrined in the Method. This is a key moment in the modern history of acting.

Streetcar had come to the London stage after New York, and Olivier had directed Leigh as Blanche (Bonar Colleano had played Stanley—how famous is he?). That production had not gone well, and some of the blame fell on Olivier's failure to grasp the play or handle Vivien. But when the movie of *Streetcar* came in sight, Kazan and Warner Brothers replaced the Broadway Blanche, Jessica Tandy, with Leigh, while making it clear to her that she was going to have to free herself from Olivier's approach to the part and be American. The film was made, no matter that Vivien Leigh's mental health was greatly stressed by it, and the actress won that second Oscar. So she was a wreck, but she was ahead again.

It was to accompany his wife to Hollywood that Olivier agreed to play Hurstwood in *Carrie,* working for director William Wyler and with actress Jennifer Jones. Adapted from Dreiser's novel, this is the story of a restaurant manager, unhappily married, with grown children, who ruins himself by having an affair with Carrie, a would-be actress. It was the closest Olivier had then come to playing a failure, and it is the great part in his collection that few know. One day, Kazan—a pioneer of inwardness in American acting—happened to see (or spy on) Olivier preparing Hurstwood. His account is fascinating:

> Some great actors imitate the outside and "work in" from there. Larry needs to know first of all how the person he's to play walks, stands, sits, dresses, concentrating on what might seem to us to be insignificant aspects of his characterization. I remember pausing outside a window late one Sunday morning and, undetected, watching Larry go through the pantomime of offering a visitor a chair. He'd try it this way, then that, looking at the guest, then at the chair, doing it with a host's flourish, doing it with a graceless gesture, then thrusting it brusquely forward—more like Hurstwood that way?— never satisfied, always seeking what would be the most revealing way to do what would be a quickly passing bit of stage business for any other actor.[18]

Kazan is admiring, yet critical, too; it's the Method scorning the English preoccupation with surfaces. But that technique was as holy to Olivier as "truth" was to Lee Strasberg. In fact, Olivier had read Stanislavsky in the 1920s, without being convinced. He suffered from Paula Strasberg's relentless "coaching" of Marilyn Monroe during *The Sleeping Prince*. And he had a sturdy hostility to it all: "My opinion of [Strasberg's] school is that it did more harm than good to his students and that his influence on the American theatre was misapplied. Deliberately atechnical, his method offered instead an all-consuming passion for reality, and if you did not feel attuned to exactly the right images that would make you believe that you were actually *it* and *it* was actually going on, you might as well forget about the scene altogether."[19]

In other words, the notion that the actor had become the real thing might be sentimental and simpleminded, and an evasion of the more paradoxical principle: that you had to be real and fake, at the same time. Hurstwood is a gentleman in Carrie's youthful eyes, but not quite the real thing. He has no money and no confidence. He is handsome, urbane—like any maître d'— but he is deferential, at the service of others, and waiting to fall. I think Olivier felt a chance to get at his own private subterfuge in the role—perhaps he was going deeper than Kazan realized. So Hurstwood is a modest step towards the wretchedness of Archie Rice, and Olivier's greater candor over his darker or more confused nature. After Archie would come so many troubled figures: his Othello, Edgar in *The Dance of Death,* Shylock, and the former actor James Tyrone in *Long Day's Journey into Night.*

Part of this is an actor growing older, and being in a position to choose more adventurous parts. But *The Entertainer* is remarkable because it was a new play, written for Olivier. In the years since, other actors have taken the part. John Slater toured it in Britain. A real music-hall comedian tried the part, Max Wall. Peter Bowles, Corin Redgrave, and Robert Lindsay took shots at it, without really lodging in the memory. Jack Lemmon played an American Archie in 1976 for television in a version set during the Second World War. Michael Gambon tried it in the Performance series in 1993, with Billie Whitelaw as the wife. Gambon seems well cast in that his power can cloak malice and nastiness, even if it might be hard for Gambon to be as reptilian or defeated as Olivier managed. Then Bill Nighy did it for radio, and his palpable insecurity and brittle classlessness is very promising casting. But casting is not the same as having a play written for you.

More than fifty years after the premiere, Archie Rice still belongs to Olivier even if our knowledge of this is no more than a still, or the memory of a movie moment. If the play is not good enough to be revived, then it will increasingly be rated as more Olivier than John Osborne. Many of Olivier's performances must take their place in the history of performance, and so our great Hamlets or Lears have company. But sometimes, one way or another, a role is never separated from a particular actor. Say "Harvey" now, and those who remember respond "James Stewart," talking to an invisible rabbit in the movie, though Frank Fay created the part on stage, with huge success (and more than seventeen hundred performances). That happens more in movies —so Norman Bates *is* Anthony Perkins, and usurpers or sharers have a hard time. Vivien Leigh is Scarlett O'Hara, and any subsequent attempt risks weary mockery. On stage, such parts are rarer. Already we have a team of Stanleys and Blanche DuBois. But Archie speaks to a moment in British history when the imperial bedrock was cracking and a famous actor felt the appealing risk in discarding his own heroic aplomb. And when he bumped into a writer prepared to teach him a lesson.

■

"A company of actors"—it is an encouraging professional phrase, from which one can easily picture the company as a willing and loyal team, collaborating in the presentation of a play. The phrase is also a metaphor for any human gathering, or for any departure from solitariness. Thus it is a way of suggesting that, gathered together in their urge to communicate, people will perform, pretend, exaggerate, lie—all to the fine ends of "company." How easily the language of theatre applies to regular, amateur life.

We have to imagine that one day, or one millennium, in the gradually emerging thing to be called society, men and women began to act. Instead of just being themselves, they presented those selves with some sort of purpose. But at first, to act is simply to do something, to perform an action or report a thing that has happened. So let us say that a tribesman encountered a lion one day on the veldt. Unable to escape, he grappled with the beast. He was terribly wounded, but he was able to kill the lion. He staggered away from that conflict and found a female tribesman who was in the company of another male. They remarked on our hero's wounds. They sighed, they groaned, they howled at the blood—who knows what they did? So the tribesman enacted the fight with the lion. He may have imitated the sounds of the beast and found a cry that helped form the word "lion"—in the places where lions are still found on earth, the word for "lion" is "simba," the name of the animal in the musical *The Lion King*.

The tribesman was dying—storytellers always are, and it is what motivates them. So he let fancy add to the enactment. He made himself a little more the hero than the lion had noticed. The female put her hand on his bloody face. Was it a smile she saw? She drew a picture on the cave wall of him fighting the lion. And gradually as language formed, a legend, or a myth of the "lion-killer" came into being. Centuries later, Britain would have a king, "Richard the Lion Heart." In the Bible, the young Samson kills a lion, and that became both a painting by Cranach and a scene in Cecil B. DeMille's film *Samson and Delilah* (though that involved Victor Mature wrestling with a stuffed lion suit). Ernest Hemingway mythologized the body of a lion in "The Snows of Kilimanjaro" just as he posed with the corpse of a lion he had shot in Africa in the 1930s. He let his hair and his beard grow long as marks of manhood or manehood. These are all acts and actions in which matters of fact are married to storytelling.

In any history of how acting matters, it's fundamental that acting out began as a longing to communicate and a need to impress—and we should admit that that mix-up is not necessarily helpful to the cause of accuracy.

From reporting adventures and triumphs to the making of plays and movies is not so large a step, even if many thousand years seem to separate the two. In our history, we have so many thousands of years empty and available it can be daunting. (The cave paintings at Lascaux are thought to be a little more than seventeen thousand years old.) That step is short, as witness the candid, if not earnest, encouragement of Gary Cooper to a screenwriter in the late 1930s: "It seems to work best if you make me the hero."

Now, such remarks, especially when offered without obvious irony, can help spread the legend of vanity and foolishness in actors. But the writer Cooper was advising, Niven Busch, noted that the scheme was sound, and that it did bring a hesitant script to life (it was for a film called *The Westerner*). Actors do like to look good: that often means to be good-looking, but just to be looked at can be enough. So actors presented with new scripts often limit their reading to their own roles—*please highlight that in yellow.* They like screen time and close-ups; they have acquired the innate ability to upstage others in a play; they expect above-the-title credits and the most money. They will require the attention of strangers even if their response suggests that it wearies and dismays them.

In twenty thousand years, say, the actor has gone from being an unnamed Goth or a tribesman to the Laurence Olivier who, in 1956, consented to have a cigarette named after him. It was all the things he wanted to be: smooth, cool, refined, sophisticated, and the packaging and advertising used dark blue and gold to remind smokers of his naval service. Quite quickly, he found that he was earning more than £3,000 a year in royalties on the cigarettes (on sales of more than 400 million).[20] By the time of *The Entertainer,* Sir Laurence Olivier was an icon of smart ease as well as one of the most admired people in Britain. His marriage to Vivien Leigh helped in that. But at that very moment he was having to admit that he did not love Vivien any longer. He would write in his autobiography about having to play the part of beloved:

> The fact was I couldn't move; it would be some time before I could entirely take it in, grasp it, or wholly believe it. My recent knighthood, bestowed just before I set out for Australia, was sacred to me too; I just could not bring myself to offer people such crude disillusionment. I could only keep it bottled up in myself and, as Vivien

had suggested, carry on as if nothing had happened. Brother and sister; ho, hum.

Somewhat to my surprise, occasional acts of incest were not discouraged. I supposed I would learn to endure this coldly strange life, so long as I never looked to be happy again.[21]

Some actors want to be heroes; others are content not to seem like the messes they may be in reality. Brando and Philip Seymour Hoffman seemed to live with that untidiness. Brando "let himself go," while Hoffman seemed determined not to look like an actor. The more famous they became, the more troubled they seemed to be. The private life of Larry and Vivien was melodrama much of the time. Vivien Leigh (and her mother) had ordered Dorothy Tutin to appear before them to be questioned. They then warned Tutin off and told her that she had no future with Larry without Vivien killing herself. Tutin was alarmed, and then in a while Joan Plowright began to be the instrument over which Olivier and Leigh might break up. The settlement of that rupture seems to have occurred in New York, at the Algonquin, where the lovers stayed during the successful run of *The Entertainer.*[22]

■

It is a fancy to imagine tribesmen or cave dwellers returning from the veldt or the swamp and telling stories about it, reenacting what transpired. But something like that happened, perhaps with the storytellers near death and acting out their demise. What is just as interesting is to wonder at the evolutionary process whereby the returning tribesman thought to himself as he limped home—well, what am I going to say, or what am I going to do to act out the adventure? How can I explain why I didn't catch anything?

When did he see that as a storyteller he controlled the process? The people "at home" were likely to believe whatever he said. So, sooner or later—ten thousand years here or there—he saw the possibility of being amusing about it: "There were these five lions but they couldn't decide which of them deserved me, so they argued, and the more they discussed it the sadder they became, so I escaped. Lions are all very well, but they're idiots." And once our archetype had felt the edge that we call humor now, then surely he realized he could tell the story for comic effect. He might even lie—with the kindest of intentions. By then, he had identified the function and the personality of acting. He was playing with himself.

The persona has taken different forms over the ages, and in different cultures, but the actor is often said to be a shady or disreputable character—and that's the liberty Olivier found in Archie Rice. Why should that be when musicians seem to have earned more natural respect? In Greek theatre, most actors wore masks that signaled and codified the nature of their roles, but which also suggested that the personalities of the individual actors were not relevant to the story they were telling. They were vehicles, or the lines on which the vehicles ran.

To this day, in concert music, the face of the player is rather overlooked, or discounted (not that anyone has quite managed that with Anne-Sophie Mutter and a few others; not that Leonard Bernstein ever gave up on the role of "Lenny"). But the face concentrating on the music and the playing is not required to be "good-looking." A similar tradition has applied to opera, where leading roles are often enough played by out-of-shape bodies and homely faces that do not detract from the beauty of the voices and the music.

To judge by the inches of press coverage, we still believe that actors are more interesting in interview than musicians. (I fear the opposite is true—many actors are dull without scripts, especially the devout improvisers.) We have yielded to glamour or attractiveness, or is it even "personality" in actors? And that indicates the suppression of those things when actors wore masks. So Greek actors were non-people, delivering the tragic eloquence of Sophocles, Aeschylus, and Euripides. They were singing the speeches rather than making them naturalistic. We have heard of a few of the Greek actors—like Thespis—but the plays remain vivid while the actors are eclipsed. So it was natural that actors be treated like people with no identity or claim on posterity.

Worse was to follow—and still endures. By the era of Roman theatre, the masks had been abandoned, along with much clothing. Actors were bawdy, pretty, and licentious, and despised for it even if they were "entertaining." The players were poor, itinerant, and lower class—to this day people in theatre (often broke and out of work) like to speak of themselves as "gypsies," and that classic musical *Gypsy* is a cry from the heart that outcasts be made whole, rich, famous, and glorified. There is a folklore in which itinerant actors leave with rent unpaid and recent friends pregnant. In Jean-Luc Godard's film *Vivre Sa Vie,* Nana wants to be an actress. When that fails she slips into prostitution. To appeal to the public can lead to servitude and obedience. Gore Vidal warned of the inadvisability of electing a president who had been raised by being told where to stand and what to say, and whose "character" had been bought with wages.

Acting is better organized than it has ever been, but the glory and the income are not widespread. It is a commonplace of our culture that young men and women who become actors are making a sacrifice of themselves. They face the humiliating ordeal of having to audition, and being refused. Until you have auditioned, you do not know the courage it takes to be scorned and humiliated—sometimes four times a day. Young actors may be exploited financially and sexually; or they may never get a chance to show us all, and themselves, whether they can do it. The extremes of this gamble exist in the universality of a Johnny Depp, his immense income and the legend of what his charm can do for his private life. But for every Depp there are thousands who will die in poverty, outside the alleged safety nets of society. Of course, the preconception was always there that actors are not reliable as people, and will come to bitter ends. From Canio in *Pagliacci* to Chaplin's Calvero in *Limelight,* the player is victim to the form.

As actors became celebrities, in the age of movies, so the habits of young, often uneducated beauties with sudden money added to the dark portrait of acting. They were figureheads in the onset of divorce; they were the earliest notorious drug takers, the spendthrifts and the show-offs. Actors, or stars, were resented by the very people whose adulation had made them famous. In time, it became clear that some of these stars had to burn out or fall to satisfy the envy and the resentment of the unknown masses. All of that increased the contempt accorded actors. So today, millions of people are likely to sneer at the mere mention of "Lindsay Lohan" (among others) without knowing enough about her. Thus her act and her publicity have to be worthy of scandal and rebuke.

But beneath the layers of gossip and ill-report there exists a suspicion that informs our appreciation of actors. We believe that these people are gentle liars and addicted pretenders. And in making these assumptions, we infer that the "others," the audience, are sober, honest, down-to-earth citizens whose worst instincts for dishonesty are exercised and even exorcised by the actors. Actors are the spokesmen for fiction itself in a world where we cling to the myth of fact.

Nothing makes this clearer than the early death of exceptional actors. In sixty years, the legend of James Dean has not diminished, and it is armored against any real boredom and waywardness he felt by the time of his sudden demise. Dean had done so little work that his meaning is irresistible. Unexpectedly dead at forty-six, Philip Seymour Hoffman had worked so hard that he might have seemed dedicated, professional, and tireless. He died by mishap, even if the accident was in line with his addictive personality (work is an addiction). But instantly the rare pain in so many of his roles took precedence and became an explanation of the man. The curtain makes any last line a verdict. Hoffman's life had turned into a story, and an example. You could labor ten years to describe his real life of turmoil and persistence, but it would barely touch his inadvertent drama. The death became his last work.

■

Only a few years before the birth of William Shakespeare, in 1564, the Marian persecutions had seen the execution and burning of many Protestant "heretics" in Britain. That spirit of hostility did not stop with the accession of Elizabeth I, even if she took a more pragmatic attitude to religious dissent. Elizabeth's reign reached a climax in the defeat of the Armada, an attempt to regain Britain for the Catholic faith. The eventual execution of Mary Queen of Scots would not have occurred had she not been a Catholic. Roman priests in England were pursued and eliminated. Many of the great country houses had "priests' holes" and secret chapels to avoid that fate. It was an age of fierce doctrinal attachments, and of conflicting faiths, all of which might be the stuff of drama. Yet Shakespeare's work does not contain one character notable for his or her faith. Cardinal Wolsey is a leading character and an ecclesiastical authority in *King Henry VIII,* but he is an entirely cynical figure.

It is not that Shakespeare was unaware of the religious currents of his time. There is even some evidence that his family was Catholic. But the fusion of drama, emotion, and intellect that we think of as "Shakespearean" is still humane, skeptical, and atheistic. The most remarkable sign of modernity in his work is the sudden grasp of an existential loneliness full of the confusion between a person and an actor. No one in Shakespeare trusts any faith but selfhood and performance.

Hamlet is a play in which actors are significant characters, and where most characters can be seen as actors. The players who come to Elsinore are like the acting companies Shakespeare knew in London. If one cares to analyze Shakespeare's work to discover who he might have been, the Players scene speaks to the man who had enjoyed the company of actors. Moreover, it has been observed that the longer someone is an actor the less likely he or she is to tolerate or require other company. More than a profession, it is like a conspiracy or a closed family in which actors marry one another, are unfaithful with other players, and seem to find no other company endurable. It is as if they breathed an air sustained by their own gatherings. So Hamlet is only at ease with the Players. On a rewrite there should be a subtext urging him to go away with them and abandon Denmark.

From the outset, Hamlet is a man lost in the attempt to play himself, and never certain about his own sanity. It is not that he cannot act, but that he cannot help but see anything he does as a theatrical gesture. "To be or not to be" sounds like life in the balance, but it is also a metaphor for an actor having to choose. Does he see the ghost of his father, or does he want to see it? *Hamlet* is not just a play that believes in ghosts; rather, it believes in that part of ourselves ready to succumb to them.

Hamlet has gathered its many ghosts over the years. In 1989, Daniel Day-Lewis took on the role at the National Theatre in London, with Richard Eyre directing. That casting was a coup, for Day-Lewis was at his first peak. Several remarkable stage appearances had been sharpened by his movie career, and he had just won his first Oscar as Christy Brown in *My Left Foot*. For that picture, he had become Brown for the duration of the shooting: he pretended to be crippled by cerebral palsy so that he had to use a wheelchair—the crew members grew bitter about lifting him here and there. He elected not to speak, except in the very limited ways available to Christy. Was he in control of this immersion, or was there a point at which he became its sea creature?

Are we in control of the life we are leading, or does it occasionally run away with us? One reason we love actors is because we are so understanding of their professional predicament.

In addition, by 1989 Day-Lewis was fretting in his new celebrity status. He was in a relationship with the French actress Isabelle Adjani, not known for a calm temperament. And then came *Hamlet*. It was one thing to embody a semicoherent paraplegic, and maybe a tougher test to become Hamlet. But Day-Lewis made that venture, and he was increasingly fixed on the idea of a young man who sees the ghost of his father. Daniel's own father, the poet Cecil Day-Lewis, had died when the son was fifteen. Daniel had never studied at the Actors Studio, but he had grown up affected by Method actors. He took on the agony of Hamlet for himself—as Lee Strasberg would have advised, he found the prince in himself.

The play opened and was poorly reviewed, sometimes by critics who attacked him for being "a film actor." Some felt that Day-Lewis was not "reaching" people. He became distressed, and this rose to such a pitch that in one performance Day-Lewis started to sob on stage. That could still have been Hamlet—the text can absorb some improv. But then the actor left the stage and took the role with him. He could not return. Jeremy Northam (who had been playing Osric) took over and performed brilliantly. In the heat of the moment, Day-Lewis said (or believed) he had seen the ghost of his father on stage. In Ingmar Bergman's great film *Persona,* Liv Ullmann plays an actress, Elisabet Vogler. One night, playing *Electra,* she is struck dumb on the stage. That silence prompts her "retirement" to an island with a nurse (Bibi Andersson) . . . the film is *begun.*

Richard Eyre was directing the Day-Lewis *Hamlet,* and he felt he had failed his actor. For Eyre, it was the process and the play that had been overwhelming:

> When [Day-Lewis] left the stage in the middle of the scene with the Ghost, it was because, with his remorselessly punishing honesty, there was nothing else he could do. His problem was not so much his relationship with the Ghost of his father, as his relationship with the play. He wrestled nightly with its subjects—fathers, mothers, sons, grief, suicide, sex, love, revenge, intellect, violence, pacifism, discipline, and death and if they floored him he was guilty not of neurosis or incompetence, but of an excess of ambition.[23]

That is generous, but insightful, too, and it leads us to this challenging brink: if Day-Lewis had to escape that stage, perhaps Hamlet is compelled to quit Denmark. He does try. But here we are close to a disconcerting prospect: that an actor is so intensely "in" a play that he has to rewrite it? Any novelist struggling with his story knows this temptation and regards the chance that the story one day will be read, settled, and a classic with terrible, ruinous mockery.

Why shouldn't Day-Lewis feel he was Hamlet? Isn't that the point of the exercise? Isn't that the magic we have paid for? Years later, he moderated his opinion of what had happened. Why not? He was older, calmer perhaps, and able to regard the furies of youth from a distance.

> I may have said a lot of things in the aftermath, and to some extent I probably saw my father's ghost every night, because of course if you're working in a play like *Hamlet* you explore everything through your own experience. . . . So yes, of course, it was communication with my own dead father, but I don't remember seeing any ghosts of my father on that dreadful night.[24]

This all seems understandable. I daresay most of us see or "see" our lost parents several times in a week. We wonder what would they say? We may talk to them in ways we never quite managed while they were alive. Why not? Aren't we all developing our part? But Day-Lewis, talking in 2012, still recalled "that dreadful night" and the crisis that removed him from that production. He was replaced with Ian Charleson, and then Jeremy Northam came back when Charleson fell ill. Day-Lewis went on, and on—*The Last of the Mohicans, The Age of Innocence, In the Name of the Father, Gangs of New York, There Will Be Blood, Lincoln* . . . He is as good an actor as we have now. But he did not return to *Hamlet,* and he has never again appeared on stage.

Hamlet is playwright and director. He guesses at a plot between his mother and his uncle, but he has difficulty mustering the will to act upon it. Increasingly paranoid in the court at Elsinore, he regards so many people as ploys meant to trap him—Rosencrantz and Guildenstern, Polonius, and even Ophelia. Thinking that they are wondering whether he is mad, he sometimes pretends to insanity with reckless and contradictory statements. Today we read that as characteristic of a bipolar personality—as if the act of madness could ward off the dread condition. Hamlet employs the Players to put on a melodrama that may catch Claudius and Gertrude, and the play leads to a reenactment of the family tragedy in which murder and accidental death solve the real mystery. The melodrama destroys Hamlet himself, yet sets him free in a version of courage in action—the duelist who will root out corruption. The self-dramatist finds his way to self-destruction. Beyond his one friend, Horatio, and the professional companionship of the Players, he will find only one other familiar, the skull of Yorick, the jester from the old court:

> Alas, poor Yorick! I knew him, Horatio: a fellow of infinite jest, of most excellent fancy; he hath borne me on his back a thousand times and now, how abhorred in my imagination it is! My gorge rises at it. Here hung those lips that I have kissed I know not how oft. Where be your gibes now? Your gambols? Your songs? Your flashes of merriment, that were wont to set the table on a roar?

That comes at the start of the last act, and denotes a calmer Hamlet, who foresees his own death in the skull and is struck by the gap between life and the merely lifelike. There is a hushed horror in the prince; he has come out on the other side of madness, but recognizes the trap he has been in between himself and its acted version. At such moments *Hamlet* is not just a nightmare of incest or the dread of taking action, but an entire metaphor for the presentation of self. *Hamlet* endures and increases the more we learn about the duplicity of selfhood. It is a play about theatre and our failure to exist as more than amateurs playing ourselves. The question that hangs over it is less who wrote it than what revelations of the brain and personality are yet to come to give it greater depth. How did anyone so long ago know us so well?

Olivier first played Hamlet in 1937. He was stimulated by Dover Wilson's recent book *What Happens in Hamlet,* and by Ernest Jones's elucidation of Freud's view of Hamlet as the victim of an Oedipus complex. But he admitted later an extra impulse in his conception of the part:

> There is another important factor in the character-drawing—his weakness for dramatics. This would be reasonable if the dramatics spurred him to action, but unfortunately they help to delay it. It is as if his shows of temperament not only exhaust him but give him relief from his absorption in his purpose—like an actor who, having spent his all in rehearsal, feels it almost redundant to go through with the performance.[25]

Brando and Seymour Hoffman never played Hamlet—except in their private chambers, perhaps. Brando had his chance. Hoffman? I don't know. But, if I may put it this way, one day after his death, a mere nod of assent would have got him the part, with whatever production and cast he liked, and the guarantee of packed houses. Alas, *Hamlet* is a play about ghostliness.

Once one has this way of looking at Shakespeare, hardly any character stands as a simple or intact being. The idea of kingship in the Histories and the uneasiness of him who wears the crown has little to do with divine right. It is a matter of political assertion (self-casting) and then carrying off the role. The young Hal has seemed a natural companion to Falstaff and his cronies, but then he stands up against them on being recast as king. Falstaff's heart is broken. He is a boozer, a liar, and a braggart, but he is an honest man. Hal will become the King Henry who delivers fully loaded patriotic speeches but then puts on a cloak and passes through his own nocturnal camp, a stranger, or "a little touch of Harry in the night." Thus, when it suits him, he is inclined to go back to the naturalness of his days with Falstaff.

In *King Lear,* the old man has become an idiot: he cannot tell the difference between the dishonest affection offered by Regan and Goneril from the true but understated love of Cordelia. Thus the king of Britain is reduced to a naked forked animal on the heath, the least of commoners, and a man who is now educated by his Fool. Whenever the natural order is threatened in Shakespeare, so the confrontation of man and actor comes into play. He specializes in a brand of triumphant pretender, villains but men who exult in playacting. In *Lear,* Edmund, with his plea "God stand up for bastards," is recommending his life of deception. In *Richard III* the warped figure of Gloucester revels in a direct confession of his trickery. And most of all, in Iago (Orson Welles, for one, felt the play should be called *Iago*), we have a man who is as much driven by the fervor for mischievous lying as he is by racism, sexual jealousy, or envy of Othello. These characters are inspired by their own skill in performance, and in the case of Iago many scholars have agreed that the purpose in the play is thrown off by the liberated pretender. Iago makes evil for its own sake, and because it is there, just as sharp and dangerous as a dagger that an assassin might see before his eyes. He is the playmaker.

In the Comedies, disguise and masquerade run rife. Titania falls for an ass in *Midsummer Night's Dream* and the entire scheme of romantic destiny is up in the air because of the way lovers can hardly recognize their mates. In *Twelfth Night,* the mounting confusion among Viola, Cesario, Orsino, and Olivia is surely a commentary on a way of performing in which boys usually played female roles. (We tend to look on that as a handicap for early theatre, but when we see an actor like Mark Rylance playing Olivia in *Twelfth Night,* or Vanessa Redgrave as Prospero, then we recognize Shakespeare's intuition about gender disarray. Don't forget the extraordinary Redgrave on television in *Second Serve,* the Renee Richards story.) The masquerades are comic, but they can be cruel, too—Malvolio is abused and humiliated in another subterfuge in the same play. In *A Winter's Tale,* Leontes imposes role playing on his wife, Hermione, and then leaps at the jealous conclusion that the role is her true self. He loses her until, as if by magic, the statue of Hermione comes back to life—the role becomes fresh again, and love resumes.

We can refer to this as stagecraft in a forest of mistaken identities, with plenty of official or unofficial jesters, or figures who have a right to comment on the action, like teachers or directors—Feste, Autolycus, the Fool in *Lear,* and the schematic division of Prospero's powers into Ariel and Caliban. And as stagecraft it works very well. But the deeper resonance of all this allusion to acting is in the constant use of metaphor and one thing being likened to another. What makes Shakespeare the writer he is—and an inexplicable phenomenon—is this uncanny marriage of dramatic interaction and poetic transformation. This is nature in flux. The light changes. Winter becomes summer. Birnham Wood comes to Dunsinane. Youth is preparing for age. And every person is capable of becoming someone else, and playing that part with passion. But the constant energy of the passion is the pregnancy in the poetry, or waiting for one thing to become another. Finally, acting is nothing less than a description of the struggle between life and death, right and wrong, truth and dream. Shakespeare is generally a moral being. He believes in our hope for right and truth. But he is enough in the company of actors to know the inescapable volatility, the dynamic of change.

The result is a close-run thing. In *The Tempest,* the storm could destroy the island, but Prospero is led away from magic to the freeing of Ariel and Caliban. In *Othello,* the facts are cleared up by the end of the play, and Iago's wickedness ends in accusation, torture perhaps, and death. But he refuses to explain himself: that is his last power. And so Iago's persistent, dark charm lingers. It is well to remember the opening of Orson Welles's film *Othello,* where Iago is the only one of the three main characters left alive, in a cage strung up from a wall, an imprisoned hawk surveying the ruins he has made.

Nothing in Olivier's *Henry V* relates to these considerations better than that instant in the wings of the Globe when we see the nervous actor preparing to be the King. It is very short-lived, but it may be Olivier's most significant addition to the play, and the best evidence of how making a movie had stirred him. More than sixty years later, it is easier for us to imagine that player and his awkward real life. He is married, let us say, with a couple of young children; but he has another romantic involvement—

with a young woman who makes his costumes, perhaps, the mistress of the codpiece—so that his regular life is chaotic, just waiting for the few hours of mercy and calm on the Globe stage, when his lines and the sweet arrangement of the play all fall into place. I know, this sounds too close for comfort to *Shakespeare in Love,* but one reason that lightweight picture was such a success was in divining the show behind the show, and that is one fruit of Shakespeare's sensibility. When he detected how a few steps into the limelight can carry a flawed soul into poetry and performance, why is it far-fetched to think that Shakespeare guessed at the special perspective on theatre, and its metaphor for life?

On stage or film, in dance, opera, or the commotion of sport, actors or players or performers (the words are interchangeable) can move thousands or millions of strangers in ways they will never understand. In Frank Capra's *Meet John Doe,* which is a great mess of a film, there are moments when through tiny, almost instinctive gestures or smothered glances, Gary Cooper comes as close as a movie actor ever did to capturing the ordeal of being an American hero or an ordinary guy. But there's no hint that he understood this, and every fear that he might have become stilted or self-conscious if he had grasped it. The actor does not always know what he is doing, not if he seeks to match life.

In the long run of Olivier's *Othello,* in 1964–65, in the midst of critical acclaim and sold-out houses, there was one night when some people on stage or off felt that the actor had exceeded his own limits and found something in Othello that was unique even for him—call it passion, conviction, intensity, magic, or the original (all those words are part of criticism's laborious attempts to keep up with acting). In short, several people noticed that something extraordinary was happening that night. Which does not mean that everyone noticed, or that there was a thermometer in the theatre that went over 100 degrees.

But at the end of the performance one or two people greeted Olivier in his dressing room. "Larry," they said, "that was beyond anything. But what did you do?" To which, the story goes—and it was a story that the actor told as well as his fellows—Olivier responded in joyful anguish, "I know! But what was it? What *did* I do?"

Now, Olivier was a canny self-promoter, no matter that his public acknowledged his eminence. He was also a man who believed in magic and spontaneity and chance. His doubt could be delight, as well as bewilderment. This testifies to some wonder that all actors hope for—a far side of the rainbow or the horizon where epiphany waits, identifiable in its very elusiveness. In the same way, spectators sometimes noticed that Cruyff or Pelé, Best or Maradona did things on the soccer field that were uncanny. The television camera could record them. If you wished, you could analyze the movements, like notating dance—of course, that perfect night of *Othello* went unrecorded, along with the majority of theatrical performances. But even if that night was on film, along with Cruyff's swerves and reverses, that would not be enough—because neither Olivier nor Cruyff quite knew what he was going to do until he had done it. And then it was too late. Plenty of actors will say they can do nothing but prepare themselves, and wait for a magnificent accident to occur.

This marriage of grandeur and the commonplace pervades the history of acting: it's the secret to how actors can seem great yet ordinary in a role, and why we are in dangerous waters if we ever worship or fall in love with them. You can have sex with a player (you should; they expect it), but give them your best and deepest self, and they may turn into a casual passerby. For his exemplary biography of Olivier, Terry Coleman interviewed Peter Hiley, who had worked as an assistant to the great man. Very often it is such people—secretaries, dressers, drivers, or servants—who have better insight into actors than other players. Hiley worked with Olivier for twelve years and he said this:

> What I felt about Larry is that he was a giant in show business, *the giant*. But as a man he was very light. Vivien was not light in that way at all. From one room to another he could switch his temperament. This is one of the actor's great talents. He treated serious things very lightly. He had a great sense of black humour. He was not a deep man. Vivien was a very strong woman, very intelligent, very streetwise, very generous. Larry was not really interested in people, you see. He would observe someone, thinking that would make a good something for Shylock, but he was picking up mannerisms; he wasn't wondering what that person was like. He was a very light, amusing man, and he was very patient. . . . He hated being alone, and if he was going to eat in a restaurant someone was dragged along, and you could have a perfectly ordinary conversation as if he wasn't the greatest actor in the world.[26]

Suppose that is the bargain, or the contract—and not just with Olivier. Suppose you are in possession of a light, chatty Olivier for small public occasions—that man who can smack his brow and cry out, "My God, what *did* I do?" I am not making a mockery of him. But the amazement is itself a show, and part of a haunting failure to be simple and real. For he is always likely to turn his companions into an audience.

He wanted to be loved, and admired. He wanted applause. And he guessed he was an awful person. The marriage to Vivien Leigh had been an infatuation, and then it was a career move, no matter the rivalries that sprang up. Both partners sought sexual adventures outside the union. Leigh had her flagrant affair with Peter Finch that was an affront to the light, easygoing Olivier. He had his secret affair with Dorothy Tutin. Then along came Joan Plowright. But even as he had just had a child by Plowright, Olivier had a brief affair with the twenty-year-old Sarah Miles during the filming of *Term of Trial*. She was there, and she revered him, and she was as sexy as could be. She was a ball that a George Best could not help playing with. Miles would say that Olivier needed to prove his virility and his guilt over Vivien.[27] But even when the divorce from Leigh was finalized, Olivier wrote to her (again, it is quoted in Terry Coleman's book). This was the day after the divorce hearing, and surely it is a magical performance, the enactment of metaphor and "I wish," but a little queasy:

> Darling, This is awky to write you will understand. But I know what horror it must have been for you, and I want to say thank you for undergoing it all for my sake. You did nobly and bravely and beautifully and I am very oh so sorry that it must have been such hell to you, and I am dearly grateful to you for enduring it and setting me free to enjoy what is infinitely happy for me. Oh God Vivling how I do pray that you will find happiness and contentment now. I pray that I may take off from you some of your unhappiness on to myself and I must say it seems to work from this end as your unhappiness

is a torment to me; and the thought of it a constant nightmare. Perhaps now it may be allowed to gently lift off and blow softly away. That's all for now.[28]

Is there an unconscious pastiche of Shakespearean verse there? (Both Olivier and Welles could turn on the Bardic faucet.) Plus, if acting matters because it can illuminate the depth in life, don't forget that it also condones or enables bad behavior.

ACT **II**

Twilight

The dining room. Saturday 6 P.M. A fine evening—sun streams through the large windows of the room. A solid table and four chairs.

Burbage Road is an ordinary street in southeast London where people take great care over ordinariness. It can carry one from out of Brixton by way of Herne Hill to the edge of Dulwich. In its way, it is a smart road, well maintained, with several desirable properties if never reaching the location value of Dulwich itself (a gem on the property market). But it has that shabby anonymous air that is generally favored in south London, as if to suggest that the secret life of the city goes on there and not in north London, which is more showy, historical and affluent. So there is no reason to suppose that many children ambling along on Burbage Road know why it is Burbage or what that might signify.

Yet Richard Burbage was an essential actor. To the best of our understanding he created several parts on the London stage: Hamlet, Othello, Richard III, and King Lear. Inasmuch as he was a leading member of the Lord Chamberlain's Men, it is possible that he played the part of Henry V in what was probably its first performance at the new Globe Theatre. So he is the leading bet for the original of that actor in the wings in the Olivier film waiting for his entrance. Furthermore, we do believe that Shakespeare himself played the part of the Chorus that day:

O for a Muse of fire, that would ascend
The brightest heaven of invention,
A kingdom for a stage, princes to act
And monarchs to behold the swelling scene!
Then should the warlike Harry, like himself,
Assume the port of Mars; and at his heels,
Leash'd in like hounds, should famine, sword and fire
Crouch for employment. But pardon, and gentles all,
The Flat unraised spirits that have dared
On this unworthy scaffold to bring forth
So great an object; can this cockpit hold
The vasty fields of France? Or may we cram
Within this Wooden O the very casques
That did affright the air at Agincourt?

Plainly, Burbage was a star. For anyone interested in wooden Os, how easy it would be to think we overhear the critics of 1599 chatting about Burbage: "His Hamlet, I thought, had a perspicacity that made his energy hard to credit—and vice versa." "Really, the day I saw him, I thought his Lear was somewhat weary—as if his Cordelia had eaten too much in rehearsal." "Ah, I think Burbage had a cold that day."

That is foolish, gentle pretending, but it does draw attention to a few valuable lessons: a great actor may have an off day, and critics may be dull. And Richard Burbage is just one of those actors about whom we know nothing of the many things for which he is known. He might as well have not been there. But if you walk a little farther in southeast London, you will come to the impressive open fields and the very decorative Italianate buildings of Dulwich College, a school founded in 1619 by one of Burbage's colleagues and rivals, Edward Alleyne, or Alleyn, or

Allen, or . . . Ben Affleck in *Shakespeare in Love* (where Martin Clunes plays Richard Burbage).

So in any consideration of acting, one has to concede the ways in which for centuries it mattered only for its moment, and as a way of inspiring word-of-mouth recommendation. But actors knew, and were accepting of the fact, that their passion evaporated. Of course, if one could have explained to Burbage and Alleyne that videotape was coming along (a blink and a half away), they might have been mortified and indignant. Or not. There is a fatalism in actors, even those who have lived in the age of recording devices, that says, "Never mind—there is something in the heart of playing that needs oblivion closing in." For instance, if your child is being born, do you want a video camera there, with a Wiseman-like operative? Or, if you are on the cliffs of Big Sur as a June sun sets, do you interrupt the experience to make sure it is properly recorded for generations yet to come (if they have the machines to play your archaic novelty)? Or are you of a mind that believes you must remember your child wriggling free from birth and staring into your face but refusing to be surprised?

In *Look, I Made a Hat,* Stephen Sondheim reports an argument he had with English theatre people over London's backwardness in not preserving stage productions on videotape:

> I was certainly aware that revisiting a show, even without any changes in the cast, sometimes constitutes an experience noticeably different from the first impression, but . . . I had never paid much attention to the implication: namely, that theater and music, unlike the printed word, the painted canvas, the building, the sculpture,

the frame of film, are ephemeral. Each performance disappears as soon as the curtain comes down or the last note fades; each audience has a unique experience and even if it's filmed it can never have its original impact again. Moreover, once a play has closed, the entire production no longer exists; the sets are burned, and the costumes as well if they don't get lent out to other productions or are taken home by the actors. All that's left is the text, which is lifeless until it's performed.[1]

We'll come back to Sondheim: he is so smart on performance, and he admits that he cannot write songs, let alone their shows, without becoming an actor. But look deeper into the lost lives of players: it is a realm so close to the forgotten existence of all of us.

Here is a story, and it was told to me by a good friend, Peter Smith, who has given years of his life to researching a book about Wilfred Lawson, to be called "The Greatest Actor of Them All." Lawson lived from 1900 to 1966. He played Doolittle in the film of *Pygmalion,* and he had a success as *The Father* by Strindberg. He was known in his time, especially in the profession, as someone capable of genius, but of being such a drunk that he could not be hired, or insured. The latter did get in the way of the former. This story occurs not long after the end of the Second World War. Lawson is strolling along Shaftesbury Avenue, still a place of many theatres, when he sees an old friend, another actor, who has been away in the war. They embrace; they find a public house. They talk. At one point, the friend asks, "Well, what's on that's worth seeing at the moment?"

Lawson mentions a play—I don't know what it was; I don't know whether this story ever happened—and says people speak well of it. So they agree to go along to that theatre and see whether they can get seats for the evening performance. They are drinking all the while.

Next, they are squeezed together in the gallery. The lights go down. It may be they have a flask of liquor with them. The play begins. They both watch with interest. Whereupon, Lawson whispers to the friend, "Something very interesting is about to happen?"

"What's that?" says the friend.

"Well," says Lawson, with unaffected curiosity, "in just a moment I am supposed to come on."

The story stops there. No one knows what happened—was there an understudy, or did the boozy Lawson stagger down from the gallery to the stage? Perhaps it's all made up. But it's a story founded in a great truth, albeit like a nightmare, of being an actor in a play where the lines, the blocking, the production simply vanish. But life waits.

In the same spirit: anyone interested in the story of acting must take a look at the movie of Olivier's *Othello*. After the reported glory of that production on stage, a plan was launched to put it on film. The sets from the stage production were kept but enlarged. The stage director, John Dexter, had Stuart Burge direct the movie. The cast was the same: Olivier, Frank Finlay as Iago, Maggie Smith as Desdemona, Joyce Redman as Emilia.

No one has questioned the film's fidelity to what was a pioneering show. So why is it not very good? On screen, Olivier in blackface, with a very calculated accent, is mannered and hard to digest. In 1964–65 the show had daring—it seemed then like an unprecedented portrayal of the blackness in Othello. Now it seems fussy and condescending. And all the old problems in that play obtrude, for surely it keeps nagging away at the possibility that it ought to be called *Iago*.

Of course, the historical value is beyond dispute. Sondheim said he would have loved to have seen the Oedipus Olivier did in 1945. All well and good, but no one is spared his Othello. It may be perverse to say this, but I don't want to see that movie of *Othello* again, whereas I would give a lot to see a recording of a version done just a few years earlier. In 1961, under the leadership of Peter Hall, John Gielgud agreed to do *Othello* at Stratford-on-Avon, despite having avoided the part for years, believing it was not suited to his nature. But now he would do it. Ian Bannen (he was playing Hamlet in the same season) would be Iago, Dorothy Tutin would be Desdemona, and Franco Zeffirelli was engaged to direct.[2]

It was very bad (so legend has it): Gielgud had been correct in thinking he was not born to the role. At one point, he was asked, to get closer to Othello, whether he had not ever known a personal moment of jealousy. "Well," he muses, "perhaps when Larry did *Hamlet*." He soon fell out with Ian Bannen, a nervy actor who favored the Actors Studio style. And Zeffirelli insisted on cumbersome sets and costumes. On opening night everything went wrong: the costumes were too heavy to wear; pieces of the set collapsed; Bannen misread a key line; Gielgud's beard came off at an intimate moment, and Tutin was trying to push it back in place. The two conventional intervals stretched out to thirty minutes each. Some critics said it was the worst thing they had ever witnessed. Critics are always saying that—or "the best."

Don't you die to see that Gielgud *Othello*? Isn't the preserved precision of a version that got everything "right" rather depressing in contrast? Or are we at a point in history when the classical status of Shakespeare almost requires an occasional disaster or the kind of terrorist assault that was made on *Hamlet* by Charles Marowitz or Steven Berkoff?

What do you know of David Garrick?[3] If you are a Londoner, you may have passed the Garrick Club (at 15 Garrick Street), which concentrates on actors and authors for its membership. There is a Garrick Theatre, on Charing Cross Road; it opened in 1889, paid for by W. S. Gilbert. You may have heard such phrases as "Garrick was the father of English acting," and there is still a general respect for his importance without any understanding of what he was like. There is a painting of Garrick, by William Hogarth, who is usually considered to be a tough, naturalistic artist. It shows Garrick playing Richard III on the eve of the battle of Bosworth Field. He wears Elizabethan costume, and he is sitting on a bed within a canopied tent. His face is pale and shocked and his right hand is raised, its fingers splayed, as if to ward off an evil spirit. It is the moment where Richard has had a nightmare about the coming battle, and the painting suggests that Garrick was arresting in this melodramatic moment. The picture is 1745, and Garrick lived from 1717 to 1779.

One thing we do know is that Garrick did a lot to organize the business. If he was a great artist, or just an artist, he seems to have guessed that the art should be businesslike. So it was that Charles Fleetwood engaged Garrick for many seasons at the Drury Lane Theatre. Garrick occupied that place for nearly thirty years, which means that he oversaw a company of players, the selection of plays, the building of scenery and the provision of costumes, and some elementary form of stage lighting. He was interested in the box office and advertising. It is even possible that Garrick may have said to Hogarth, "You could paint me?" as a way of building business.

Garrick wrote plays himself, but they have not lasted. He encouraged Shakespeare in his repertoire as well as other seventeenth-century classics. There is a vague suggestion that he urged the audience to pay attention. As to his acting, you take your pick: there is a line in the stories about Garrick that he was quiet and natural, not grandiose and flamboyant in his gestures. Some of that may be so, but in the history of acting, age after age, new wonder after new wonder, truth, human accuracy, and restraint steadily invade acting and disabuse the grand gestures that we might call overacting. So it is a history of increasing lessness and it goes on and on, yet somehow every master of underplaying looks like a ham thirty years later. There's no reason to be provoked or angry because of this. The history is a lesson for us, and we have not yet reached the crucial turning point in handling acting, when cameras suddenly revealed that many gestures of the art were insufferable and underlined. So for Garrick the naturalist there were contemporary accounts that said he was an extraordinary show-off and fusspot who could not keep his hands, his eyes, or his throbbing imagination still.

If, for the sake of argument, you want to imagine David Garrick and Marlon Brando sharing a scene in the back of a New

York city taxicab, then it's easy to think of Garrick insisting that he had always done what an older brother could and should do to look after his punch-drunk kin, beating the blinds on the back window of the cab (how was the driver expected to drive?), filling the small space with remorse, self-examination and sheer acting as vaporous as the smell of booze coming off a drunk, while Brando just watches him and sighs, and steals the scene. Acting is often a kind of cutting contest in which the fellow who does the least takes the cake. Which is not to say that in 1750 or so, David Garrick may not have been as stunning as Brando was in 1954 in *On the Waterfront.* But then you should recall that in 1954 some critics assured themselves that Brando truly had become a washed up prizefighter, Terry Malloy, a semisimpleton, even though he now looks like the most beautiful ex-boxer you ever saw and an actor of extraordinary cunning (think of his way with Eva Marie Saint's gloves!). Stephen Sondheim may say on film it is always the same performance, but that view is too limited. Once the audience grows older then the performance may shift. We are eager souls and part of a business enterprise that longs for fresh sensations (this may be Garrick's best legacy), so we are determined to be swept off our feet. It is an upheaval as wild as falling in love, and it is like the difference between an actor "resting" (as the saying goes) and being given a new part.[4]

That's when you need to recollect this terrible fact of the acting life: that the great majority of people who long to act—and it is a rare impulse, never lightly undertaken—will be denied or disappointed. They will be regarded as "failures"; they may never get a part at all. They may be the problem in their families.

There are suicides and cases of mental breakdown that are in part explained by the frustration in people who longed to act.

Imagine two young women at the age of twenty-two, both of them on the brink of determining to be an actress. The one, the more accomplished at that age, is shy, inward, rather melancholy and afraid of many things she has heard about the business of acting—not least the likelihood of failure. The other is more beautiful and more romantic about acting. The first woman decides she will not try: it will be too much for her. The risk terrifies her. So she will get married and lead what she hopes will be a happy, settled life. God knows how that turns out, and how tranquil she will ever be with the smothered impulse inside her.

The prettier of the two goes into the business. She makes a few movies in small parts; she plays good roles in provincial theatre. But as she grows older she realizes that she is not established. In fact, she is in a position where there is not enough work to support her life. Her family are dismayed. They think she is unhappy and a problem, though her optimism fights off those threats. So she begins to teach young actors and she makes a life out of that, though in the regular way of things it is not clear how she will provide for herself in old age. Sometimes it may occur to her that she could have been a wife, a mother, a doctor . . . we all play with the list of roles that might have been ours.

Marlon Brando became the most revered American actor of his age. He was adored, and he ate up the adoration in most of the ways healthy young men can find. But he was bored, too, unconvinced and never able to lose the feeling that his own great talent was foolish. Just before he made *On the Waterfront,* he played Marc Antony in a movie of *Julius Caesar.* It was the only time in his life that he would do Shakespeare. John Gielgud played Cassius, as lean and hungry as Brando was sleek. Gielgud then was close to fifty and he was embarked on a working life that only death would halt. Gielgud was a noble professional, or simply a helpless actor; it's not clear that he needed to be paid. For most actors, he was the heroic English figure of his time— even if Olivier reckoned he could beat him any night he chose to.

Gielgud was drawn to Brando, and we need not count the reasons for that. Let's just say that Gielgud could smell talent and rawness, even if its idiom and voice were unlike his own. So he did anything he could to help Brando on the film, especially in the matter of speaking the verse. The help was appreciated, and most onlookers believed it assisted Brando's Antony, which came as a pleasant surprise to those who had regarded the actor as a chronic, introspective mumbler.

When the shooting was over, Gielgud invited the young American to come to London and join him and Paul Scofield in a theatrical season. He could choose the parts he wanted to play, but Gielgud insisted that he do *Hamlet.* Brando declined the offer. In some versions of the story, he said he was going scuba diving—why not? So Gielgud shrugged. Brando went on to make *On the Waterfront,* and Gielgud returned to London. It was there, in October 1953, that he was arrested in a public lavatory for importuning. He was fined and he felt disgraced. His life carried on, but under a shadow. I do not begin to suggest that his actions were as a result of being disappointed by Brando, though dismay is a vague and far-reaching thing. We don't know where it goes or how long it remains.

Brando won the Oscar in *On the Waterfront*. He would win another in *The Godfather*. But he had his own dismay, which was that he never had Gielgud's single-minded passion for work. Brando died in 2004, a hulk, a man not working steadily. Gielgud had died in 2000, aged ninety-six, and working whenever he could. He had played the pope in *Elizabeth* the year before his death. He had trouble walking and he was short of breath, but his mind and his dedication to pretending were unaltered. How did he die? We can only imagine—that is what he taught us—and wonder whether he was like the central character in Cocteau's novel *Thomas the Impostor*, fearful in battle so that he acted brave, imagined he had been shot and then realized that life had been loaded with real bullets.

So Brando studied Antony's speeches with Gielgud, who was the grand-nephew of Ellen Terry, who died only when Gielgud was in his twenties. Terry had been the leading lady for Henry Irving's company at the Lyceum in the 1870s. Irving was taught by Samuel Phelps. It is very likely that Phelps saw Kean act— indeed, it would be fanciful to believe he missed him. Kean was somewhat opposed to but influenced by the acting style of Charles Kemble. And Kemble would have seen and been moved by David Garrick. Gielgud cherished that line.

Perhaps Terry and Gielgud felt that precious succession more than the others. They had a family tie in which the older woman valued what might be taught as much as the younger man. Early in the twentieth century, Terry played in some Shaw and Ibsen.

She made vocal recordings of some speeches. In 1906, there was a gala at the Drury Lane Theatre for her which featured Caruso, Nellie Melba, Eleanora Duse, Lillie Langtry, and Mrs. Patrick Campbell. In 1916, she made a film, *Her Greatest Performance*, and a few others, including the role of Buda the nurse in *The Bohemian Girl*, which stars Gladys Cooper and Ivor Novello. Only a part of that film survives; the recording is scratchy and archaic; there are paintings by Sargent of Terry as Lady Macbeth. But we lack her immediacy. In the years 1929–31 (in his early twenties) Gielgud himself astonished the theatre with *Richard II* and a *Hamlet* that was acclaimed as a decisive playing of the part. Nothing of either performance survives beyond still photographs and a few recorded speeches made much later. Similarly, when Gielgud and Olivier swapped the roles of Romeo and Mercutio, in 1935, when sound film was available, not a trace is left.

And so we have to imagine the contrasts in the two performances and the way they fueled the rivalry. It was accepted wisdom that Gielgud was superior in speaking the verse; he reached back into the hallowed Shakespearean tradition. But this was Olivier's first attempt at Shakespeare, and he would say, "I really was convinced that I was better in Shakespeare than John Gielgud because I didn't sing it, and my form of self praise was to pat myself on the back because I didn't sing it, because I didn't have to sing it, because I spoke Shakespeare naturally. I spoke Shakespeare as if that was the way I spoke."[5]

Olivier gave himself an extra leg up in the contest by having an affair with Peggy Ashcroft, "their" Juliet. But he is correct in that the natural or musical approach to Shakespeare was just a prelude to the tension between English and American acting, brought into being by the movies. Nothing survives except a few still photographs.

Our sense of John Barrymore is even more affected by the oddities of the times he lived in. John Sidney Blyth was born in Philadelphia in 1882, the son of and brother to actors.[6] He was exceptionally handsome, and although he was not keen to act he found himself doing witty conventional leads in minor plays. His manner and the American mood might have kept him as a light romantic actor, but he took character parts in John Galsworthy's *Justice,* and he played *Peter Ibbetson* and a version of Tolstoy. Shakespeare was not popular in America then (was it too English? too formal? too unnatural?). Whatever, Barrymore played Richard III in 1920 and then Hamlet in 1923.

Both productions traveled to England and were as highly praised in London as they had been in New York. There is no question that Barrymore was the Hamlet of his time: handsome, witty, and sarcastic in delivery, utterly sure of the virtues of the play, yet possessed by an American energy that also regarded the Dane as a sacred cow who needed to be galvanized, as if by electroshock treatment. How good was Barrymore's Hamlet? As good as Dempsey? Well, there is a kind of witness. Orson Welles admitted that as a child—he would have been eight—he stood in the wings with an iced bucket of champagne waiting for Barrymore's exits. How can you muster the sternness not to credit that?[7]

What happened with Barrymore is a portrait of a great actor

skidding on the banana skins of celebrity and personal collapse. He did not look after himself or his work. Only fragments of his Hamlet survive (silent, or throttled), but chance has kept all of his *Dr. Jekyll and Mr. Hyde* on film—an uninhibited melodrama, an escape from gravity or melancholy. Jekyll and Hyde are the mockery of immense, dignified acting: it is Hamlet inflamed with booze and making the lines up as he goes, gesturing with all the fury of silent movies. The fatalism that some had seen in his Hamlet led to such exploitation of his self, to drink and womanizing, without rest or restriction. Hollywood was the natural venue for such styles, and so Barrymore largely gave up the stage for movies, some of which are brilliant. In *Twentieth Century* he plays Oscar Jaffe, a flagrantly manipulative and self-dramatizing actor-manager at war with an equally egotistical actress (Carole Lombard), who regrets that one can have only two faces in a tight corner. As written by Ben Hecht and directed by Howard Hawks, this is one of the most joyful confessions of fraud in acting. Then in *Midnight,* Barrymore is a veteran of affairs watching and abetting the romantic intrigue of Claudette Colbert, and pricelessly comic because of his unexpected alertness to nuance and detail.

He was not out of control, as some critics alleged. One of his conquests, Mary Astor, seventeen to his forty, said he was gentle and a gentleman, easing her away from parental limitations, teaching her how to speak, and saying it was a good thing he was so much older—otherwise he would have married her. But he was not infatuated with the silly shams of masquerade; he seems to have seen through the gravity act and made his bargain with fresh whisky and attractive women. These are the roles the world has remembered, far from a Hamlet that had seemed unmatched for a few years. The camera was merciless with Barrymore: it showed what booze and dissipation had done, and how quickly. He died only a few weeks past sixty, unable to mask the glee that had driven him on. There is no self-pity or reformist instinct in John Barrymore, but every indication that when it comes to judging great actors (or trying to remember them) we should grab as many hours or scenes as possible. Late Barrymore is like W. C. Fields cut with Olivier; in fact, he is Archie Rice, but without Olivier's snob disdain. Was he rehearsing for the macabre legend of his death? The story goes that director Raoul Walsh and Fields stole Barrymore's corpse from the morgue and had it sitting up at home to face Errol Flynn when he returned from carousing. You may prefer the other report: that, after he had collapsed on the Rudy Vallee radio show, he was with his older brother, Lionel. Jack offered what were nearly dying words (and may have been intended as such). But Lionel, a little deaf, asked to have them repeated. "You heard!" snapped Barrymore.

Everyone has his or her last words of Jack Barrymore. He must have lasted days longer delivering them. His biographer Gene Fowler (*Good Night, Sweet Prince*) vowed that at the fatal moment Barrymore gave Fowler the sign that he wished to utter. Fowler dropped his head to hear and Barrymore asked, "Is it true that you are the illegitimate son of Buffalo Bill?" Spluttering with laughter, Fowler assented.[8]

These incidents place Barrymore in the line of actors giving up their own ghost, full of ghastly incredulity that anyone should believe, let alone honor, actors—he is father to his own unsteady descendants and to the self-destruction in Errol Flynn, Orson Welles, Richard Burton, Peter O'Toole, and Brando himself. In 1920 the drama critic John Mason Brown had spoken of the "lean Russian wolfhound aquilinity" of Barrymore's prince, and then Barrymore had taken pleasure in having the wolfhound succumb to one of Jekyll's transforming drugs so that he became an elderly wolf ridiculed by Red Riding Hood. In one of his last films, *The Great Profile,* he is made fun of as a legendary actor and he consented to have his character named "Garrick."

While Fredric March and Spencer Tracy made so much of the Jekyll/Hyde slippage as a feast for horror, special effects, and Robert Louis Stevenson's dread, Barrymore had foreseen how far the switch mimicked the inescapable aging process in an actor. All he had required was a little time, the feel of a slippery down-hill beneath his feet, and his own scathing wit. Barrymore was the first great actor who cried out in warning at the hubris that might abandon Blyth for Barrymore.

Just to think of the Blyth family is to face the possibility that actors cannot survive the company, let alone the "love," of any other breed but actors. John had siblings—Lionel and Ethel—and there are films, like *Rasputin and the Empress* (1932), where they can all be seen at once. (Lionel played Rasputin; John was a figure based on Prince Yusopof; and Ethel was the tsarina—fair enough, but they could have swapped roles.)

They were the children and grandchildren of actors. In turn, John had two children—Diana, who perished in her thirties from the effects of alcohol, mental disturbance, and an unsuccessful career as an actress, and John Drew, who made a few films as a young man and then turned into a recluse and a derelict who had eventually to be taken care of by his daughter, and Jack's granddaughter, Drew (born in 1975).

Drew Barrymore is the stalwart of the family, despite drug habits as a child, a suicide attempt at fourteen, and several marriages. Nevertheless, she has come through to do *The Essentials* with Robert Osborne on Turner Classic Movies, an apogee of respectable success. She has been actress, producer, director, and writer, as well as a parent, though her track record at what is known as an "ordinary human being" suggests that show people can have a hard time without lines, marks, and cues, to say nothing of the structure of dramatics and iced buckets of champagne. But Drew Barrymore has a spark of mischief enough to remind us of her grandfather's last film, *Playmates,* where he plays himself and teaches "To be or not to be" to the bandleader Kay Kyser.

At one point in that film two agents are lamenting the used-up status of this John Barrymore:

"How can I make the public Barrymore-conscious?"
"Would he marry a midget?"
"Sure, but what midget would marry *him?*"

He did a screen test for *The Man Who Came to Dinner* (at the insistence of Bette Davis) but he could not remember his lines. At public events he would use foul and abusive language and urinate on the carpet.

Of course, members of the acting profession cannot be guaranteed personal happiness in life, so they may have to be content with fictional bliss. The love between Laurence Oliver and Vivien Leigh was fairly brief in their lives, but much longer-lived in the media and in the hearts of patriots who had seen them as Nelson and Emma in *That Hamilton Woman,* and were spurred into war by it. In fact, it was not long before she—always the more candid of the two—was telling him she did not love him anymore. So they looked elsewhere (the need for new roles is oddly akin to promiscuity), and could seldom find anyone in life or in their beds who was not an actor or someone in the business. There is some reason to believe that Olivier had an affair with Danny Kaye, the comedian. They were very close, and Olivier did a few standup routines with the American clown—a hint of Archie Rice. (Kaye was married to Sylvia Fine, the woman who wrote his tongue-twister songs.) Olivier then moved to actresses, as if on the principle that if you are in search of discretion, secrecy, or lying, you might as well go for someone who has the calling. As for Leigh, actors often have a special understanding of adulterers, and spies—you can feel both in John le Carré's work, which may be the acme of one of our most guarded actors, Alec Guinness.[9]

Leigh had a long-running passion with Peter Finch. The novelist Elaine Dundy (once married to Kenneth Tynan), an observer of that union, said that the best thing to be said for Finch and Leigh was that they did very little behind Olivier's back. That could pass for a witticism, but we should allow this grain of truth: some actorly infidelities are performances, actings out, for the aggrieved party to feel bitterness over.

I have suggested that Olivier and Leigh became emotionally closer after their divorce, but that is just one more sign of the love of pretending. In person, still married, they could be very blunt. At the time of John Gielgud's arrest for importuning, a number of his friends in the business came together to plan moral support. Gielgud was about to open in a play, *A Day by the Sea,* and Olivier volunteered to have Gielgud take refuge in obscurity with Larry himself deputizing for him on stage, on book if necessary until he had the role by heart. To which Vivien responded

> You're a cunt Larry, you've always been jealous of John, and you know perfectly well that if he doesn't open in the play on Monday night, he'll never act again.[10]

How Olivier played the following seconds is one of those spasms one longs to see; it must have taken all his resources. Not that the lives of actors are always as well "written," or as pitched at the same level of melodrama. The most aggravating company that actors can keep is probably that of waiting, or "resting," together. Consider a young couple, not quite thirty, attractive both of them, with agents, and the high talk of "promise." They met at a season at the Bristol Old Vic: she was the maid in *The Country Wife* (understudying Marjorie Pinchwife), while he was Mick in *The Caretaker.* Their paths had crossed before a couple of times, but this summer in Bristol was theirs, and they were persuaded by it. Most actors are unflaggingly optimistic. You meet few who are depressive, because lacking energy is off-putting; they will go empty before they let themselves seem downcast.

They fell in love that summer and kept telling themselves

it was the real thing; and since there is no reliable test of that status, how were they to know otherwise? As it was, they were pleased with themselves. Every night there were moments when his Mick commanded the tense stage Pinter had constructed. He lost a little weight—they were having constant sex, and he had noticed that when he was unemployed he had been more inclined to snack, waiting by the phone. She was pert and droll as the maid—it is a nice, eye-catching part—and her Restoration bosoms shone in the lights. She had two nights as Marjorie, and the company said they were very impressed. There was a rumor that several London managements had been in Bristol that weekend. As if to show the company and the world their happiness and their confidence, they got married. It was one of the best parties of the season—people said that for a couple of months.

Then they noticed that they were categorized as not quite available. After all, they were together. Not that much had been going on before, but they were flirted with and they had flirted. There is a kind of careless openness in these matters in the theatre. It is like being available to be cast; no one wants to seem settled. Very little is going to happen, but people talk as if it could. It is the possibility that is appealing, that and the talk, which is loose and randy, but invariably good-natured.

"I could give you a quick one between Act Two and Act Three?"

"Don't get your Acts confused, darling."

Outsiders might hear that "darling" and read a lot into it. There's no need. It has been used for decades—maybe forever—

the way men in theatre talk, and it slides past all the silly curiosity about whether they are homosexual or whatever. As if it mattered: they are sexual, and above all they are automatically lecherous in their talk and the way they look at you. It's not personal, but an acting exercise. Mick is meant to be a sullen stud and the maid is fancied in passing by every man in *The Country Wife*. When you're that age it's nice to be noticed and to be what you can call attractive. Then one night in the wings, a stage manager whispered to her, "Isn't it great? His being offered the movie?"

"You didn't say about the movie?" she tells him that night. He is expecting to fuck her. He likes to do it after a performance, before he goes to sleep.

"It's just a stupid Tom Cruise thing," he says. "It's a shit part, but they think I'll get noticed."

"Los Angeles?" she assumes.

"And Venice," he says.

It is the first night they do not make love. He explains to her that the money is ridiculous. It's $200,000 for four weeks' work. She must come, at least to Venice. "You've never been to Venice, have you?"

She can't be sure; she refuses to be sweet and easy. There is an experimental London production from Wedekind. It's sort of *Pandora's Box*—she needs to see the movie. They have asked her about Lulu. She'll have to audition.

"You might get it?" he supposes.

"Of course, I might not. You might not get Tom Cruise."

"No, that's signed."

It is the first time she has realized he must have a secret life, so she determines all the more to get Lulu for herself. She watches the silent film, with Louise Brooks, and she is scared, but she has known that scary opportunities might come along when it was absurd to yield to fear. She might never get a chance like this again. Fuck Venice.

In a grim rehearsal room in Southwark, she auditions four times for Lulu. She has pages of stuff to learn, and then on the first day of auditions she is given fresh pages. They might be from a different play. "Should she be at all German?" she asks. And there is a crestfallen, "Oh no," as if her question was in bad taste. She does love scenes with four different men and they seem to be intent on treating her as brutally as possible—just for the part. She is hours waiting in the cold while other Lulus try out. She realizes that one of them has done a nude dance, and she asks whether she should do the same.

The director—she hasn't liked him—notices her and grins. "Want to strip off, do you?" And he's trying to be insolent and alluring at the same time. It's when being an actress is as lousy as everyone told you it might be. She guesses—she has to do it on the spur of the moment—that if she takes her clothes off she'll never get the part.

You can work out the possible scenarios. He meets someone new in Hollywood. The Lulu production is a scandal, and the actress who got the part goes into rehab. Our actress is despondent but then she is rescued by a series of commercials she does involving an amused, faintly sarcastic wife who puts up with a mindless husband but stays cute and trusts the household appliances. These ads are so remarked on that she gets a role in a new reality show. She hates all of it, because she still has Wedekind speeches in her head. But as she rises (and she is a national character for a year or two), she meets the divorced him as he sinks—no one has been able to make up their mind whether he is English or American, gay or straight. In the settlement he actually asks her for support, and her agent advises her to do it for the good copy. "Britain loves you, sweetheart," he says.

Or . . . The point here is that you could come up with eventualities for them as good, or better, just because we are like them enough to have the habit of making up possible stories. It's a way of getting through life, and it's probably the best everyday reason why acting matters. The virus is everywhere now. She gets Annie in a revival of *The Norman Conquests*—out of the blue. She wins awards. A Russian businessman in London asks her to marry him. She hears he has a wife already in Moscow. "Yes," he admits, "so . . . ?" You can do the rest.

The two actors in this scenario are not typical. They found work—on stage and screen—and in their youth, at least, they made some kind of living. Whereas the organizations that are set up to protect actors—Actors Equity and the Screen Actors Guild—admit that in any one year a majority of their members do not make money from acting work. So actors teach school (that involves playing to an audience), they wait tables, and do so many other things. Before he was one of the most successful and prosperous actors of his time Harrison Ford worked as a carpenter. There are some skills that always have a market. There may come a time when resting actors let their union membership lapse and when they are reluctant to admit in company that they once wanted to be an actor.

The common wisdom that it is a hard profession barely scratches the truth. It is not what most people would call a profession so much as an intermittent source of work but a steady means of regret or humiliation. An aging actor may gain experience, but he or she loses youth, and—just as in slavery—that is in great demand. When the young woman tried out for Lulu, there may have been sexual opportunism on the part of people behind the show. They would laugh and say she imagined it, but it would be unwise of her to pursue charges of sexual harassment. Even if she won such a case, she would be terminating her career. If she has done any research on *Pandora's Box,* she knows that Louise Brooks—who is an icon now—was once thought so "difficult" that she ran out of jobs.[11] Then she became the mistress of powerful men, and after that she lived in a small apartment in Rochester, New York, and began to write. There were decades in which the public had forgotten her. Actors frequently have had little or no health insurance, and they have not earned enough to qualify for much social security. Past a certain age, their chance of a job is remote, and they are doing what they can to survive. They probably live alone in poverty, and they have to accommodate a bitter resilience that is essential to the auditioning process.

It's not that she missed a part because she would not grant a passing sexual favor. The denial is more direct and disconcerting. She has offered her being, her hope and desire, her presence, and her imagination, and those in power have simply said, no, not you, we'll let you know—though they may not even pass along the word of refusal. An auditioning actress may be cut off in midspeech to save time; or she hears the producer and the director talking to themselves in her pauses. She sees the other people auditioning and feels herself too old, too plain, too close to being overweight. She lives by certain unbreakable principles—such as Meryl Streep's being a wonder, not just a great actress but a decent person—but she knows that for every Streep, patient at yet another nomination, there are a thousand who will die alone in a small room. And those unknowns make a bargain with themselves whereby they still believe in acting. In their scant budgets, they keep enough for television so that they can see Vanessa Redgrave do whatever oddity she does next, because they know that Redgrave's reckless and heartfelt uncertainty is the best door to acting we have, War Horse to Streep's Secretariat.

These people in their rooms are seldom depressed or cast down. (It is usually the successes who kill themselves.) That tells you as much about the importance of acting as any of Meryl Streep's best dozen golden performances. Streep knows. Every successful actor understands the odds and they cross their fingers every day.

This woman in a room of her own (so long as she has the rent) is doubly trapped by the predicament of acting. Louise Brooks eventually found a natural response to unmediated solitude: she began to write. Probably some actors have painted, or written poetry, or tried to write songs. The technical requirements for such things are very few: paper, a pencil, and time. Most arts are there for the taking. But an actor needs a company, a place, and a text—elaborate, collaborative constructs long before someone has to pay for them. Without those raw materials, the only thing an actor can do is play scenes alone in his room, or walk the streets talking the lines. We have all of us edged away from those talking people; you know the way we write them off as disturbed or troubled. As if anyone ever thought that successful actors had grown sane on the life of pretending.

There is a bittersweet irony in this situation. If you have a rich soul and I have had any skill in writing it, you have felt the pathos of this woman I have invented, caught between the moods of Virginia Woolf and Samuel Beckett. There may even have come a moment when you said to yourself—what a great part for Meryl Streep. (Don't tell herself, unless she gets excited.) But you're on to something: a woman of, say, sixty, a would-be actress who never made it, a woman you might pass on the street without paying attention, an untouched viola, a singer without a song—and maybe within and beneath it all, a very talented actress. You cannot trust that fate, chance, and the hurly-burly ensures that every significant talent sees the light of day and the limelight.

So where shall we go with this prospect? The woman at last gets an acting job? No, too obvious. Should she perform in real life? Suppose she hears of a wealthy man, so sad and reclusive he just needs a speck of company. He has never forgotten his great love from years ago—she was an adventuress lost at sea, or so it was reported. And somehow—the writers are going to have to work this out—Meryl comes back to visit him as a woman who has led an extraordinary, crowded romantic life. This encounter restores him—and herself—to life! Tell me you can't see Meryl getting a nomination with that.

Of course, nothing is new. If you think about it, Streep has come close to playing this part a couple of times already. Do you remember *Ironweed*, where she's a woman who lives on the streets, a drunk, but someone who has kept her poignant, broken singing voice? That was with Jack Nicholson, directed by Hector Babenco, from William Kennedy's novel. You can get closer with a film where Streep won an Oscar. But isn't Margaret Thatcher in *The Iron Lady* a former actress, a diva, who now lives alone in her room replaying her big scenes to the ghost of her husband and the broken lines of her memory? And don't let's have any patience with the humbug that Mrs. Thatcher was really a natural woman, instead of acting her head off. Nobody talks like that.

But actors are sometimes wary of playing actors. Is it trespassing on bad luck, or being too clever for one's own good? When Billy Wilder was trying to cast *Sunset Blvd*, both Mary Pickford and Mae West turned him down before Gloria Swanson simply possessed the courage. Were the others afraid of exposing themselves—too old, too much a has-been, too easily regarded as having been driven mad by acting? Think of the cruelty in that: ask an actress to play a crazed woman, expect her to do it every night for a year, praise her and reward her, and then suggest quietly and with sadness that she seems to have lost her mind in the process! What happened to professionalism?

This is a profound question, and a lasting paradox. Every actor wants to be in a hit, in a play that runs forever or a movie that is never forgotten. Until they feel the unyielding bonds of a very long run. Actors will sometimes say—along with critics and audiences—that they long to become the part they are playing, and regard that immersion or that loss of self as a proof of artistic resolve. But can you get back? When Vivien Leigh played Blanche DuBois on the London stage, Irene Selznick, the producer of the venture, began to fear for the actress's sanity.

Vivien Leigh had always been a perilously suggestible, romantic actress, not skilled at building a protective wall of technique or professional discipline between herself and a part. Even when she played Scarlett O'Hara in *Gone With the Wind*, the exhaustion of that arduous shoot and the intensity of her identification made some people fear for her health. Old friends passed her in the shattered fabric of Selznick's Culver City South and were not sure it was Vivien. But that had been a happy time when she was entirely in love with Olivier and guessed that the picture could make her career. By the time she played Blanche, she had admitted that she no longer loved Olivier, and she was insecure about her prowess as an actor. Olivier was directing her in *Streetcar,* while saying he didn't think much of the play. More than that, Vivien was ready to believe that she and Blanche had a danger in common—nymphomania: it was a new word, but it seemed to cover women always ready for new sexual relationships. Some friends had warned her not to play Blanche. Olivier himself was concerned that Vivien was unusually prey to taking a part home with her.

She played the role eight months on the stage and was always trembling after the last curtain when Blanche is taken off to a mental hospital. Well, of course—don't we expect great acting to be carried away at such moments? Isn't that our excitement, paid for in advance? Still, Vivien would ask friends two questions, the professional and the personal: "Was I all right?" and "Am I mad to be doing it?" On several occasions, Mrs. Selznick, her producer, had to take Vivien off for electroshock treatment, which even then was known to disturb the memory, and discombobulate the personality—as if an underground pressure was being put on the actress to speak the part from out of herself—to blurt it out, under stress—rather than trust the lines.

Once and always, it has been the custom of acting and performance for the players to call for a script. When that is settled, they learn the lines—that process fascinates nonprofessionals. It seems such a task. How do you do it? Do you ever forget? As a rule, actors do not forget. They possess their parts so thoroughly that they can then embark on the deceit or the delicacy that will let the lines sound spontaneous—as if the characters, like the rest of us in life, had just thought of what to say (on the perpetual understanding that what we say may not be the smartest thing). But then in the straining for naturalism in acting, especially in the acting associated with the Method, actors began to feel a rebellious urge. So long as they knew, more or less, what needed to be said for the plot, why shouldn't they speak freely, ad lib, or make up their own lines?

By the mid-twentieth century improvisation was being used sometimes in rehearsal, as a way of filling out the characters' lives. Many actors and directors will testify to the benefits of that approach. But once performance is reached, there are practicalities. Set lines permit cues, the signal pauses in which another character should speak. Improvisation can go "off book" or out of control. It can become the indulgence or the vanity of an actor. Marlon Brando, who had been fastidious over text during *Streetcar,* got into the habit of mistrusting lines he had to learn. So he had them written up all over the set and he sometimes had strategies like this observed by the writer Daniel Taradash on a pretty awful picture called *Morituri:*

> It was a scene with Brando and the girl in the cabin [of a ship] and there was a porthole, but the porthole was covered over because this was a ship that was not supposed to be at sea. I'm watching the scene in the projection room and Brando walks over to the porthole and looks out. Aaron [Rosenberg, the producer] says, "What in the hell is he doing that for?" Well, he went over there because the blackboard was right outside and he was trying to read his lines![12]

A great actor was by then rewriting his scripts and refusing to take direction. But you need a writer as great as Samuel Beckett to render the stupefaction and conundrum of trying to make up your mind what to say.

So many riddles about acting gather in this situation. They can sound comic in some descriptions, but don't miss the madness and the torment. For example: is it necessary for a Vivien Leigh to have been down Blanche DuBois's path in life—or is it legitimate for her to imagine it, and pretend? Is there a kind of sensationalist, voyeurist greed in us that wants Vivien in tatters every night? Should the actress be "lost" in the play's world? Does she require at least a sensible nurse and an inspired doctor? Or is it altogether more manageable if Vivien showers away Blanche's jitters, and is on display in her dressing room in fifteen minutes, sipping a cocktail, smoking an Olivier cigarette and arguing over where to go for dinner?

Suppose there's an ingénue in the dressing room that night— let's call her Eve Harrington, a would-be actress—and she says, "Oh, Miss Leigh, I believed in Blanche. I was trembling for you." And Vivien laughs the rapt compliment away, and says, "My dear, Blanche is a tough old bird. She'll still be here in twenty-five years waiting for you to play her."

"But, Miss Leigh—her desperation, her pain, her madness."

"My dear Eve," says Vivien, "do you know when I was most upset tonight? At the very point when I stepped on a nail left on the stage. It pierced my foot. *My* foot, child. Not Blanche's. So I had to be very careful not to limp!"

"Oh, that's a wonderful story," sighs Eve, and it is a story she will tell over the years (about herself).

Of course, this version of *Streetcar* casts Vivien in the mold of Margo Channing (Eve's model and then rival in *All About Eve,* a film that opened between the play and the movie of *Streetcar*). Margo is a great actress. Everyone says so—she says so. And while it's reasonable that she might offer a concession to the sentimental groundlings and let her Blanche seem like an exhausting trial that would have to pass, Margo is too interested in the bumpy nights of reality to concede a dominant place to what happens on the stage.

So is Margo a fake, or just a bit too skilled for her own good or our romantic yearnings? Set in New York, at the dawn of the

Method, *All About Eve* harks back to America's mixed feelings about the English stage. Do we feel we have been conned or exploited if Margo is so much in charge of her passion? Could Margo have played Blanche without seeming absurdly mannered and detached? It's a tempting question from a time when attitudes to acting were changing. Vivien and Blanche became a test case in which every pained account of Leigh's distress was hand-in-glove with our respect for her intensity. There are biographies that believe that in making her greatest and most dangerous experiment with herself—in becoming Blanche—Vivien Leigh deepened her own disturbance and threatened her being. But if that connection was vital and organic, would it not be possible—and even necessary—at some point for the actress to forget or abandon the Tennessee Williams text and cry out from her own fraught soul? It might even be possible (and necessary) for a young actor playing Hamlet to reach such a depth of understanding in his preparation that the words of Shakespeare become stale and false. Marlon Brando never played Hamlet, but if ever an actor might have halted in delivering that famous text, surely it was Brando, the pioneer of agonized hesitation in which nothing that can be uttered seems adequate or genuine. How can great actors know their lines—or not know them?

It is striking how far these riddles coincide with 1947: the premiere of *A Streetcar Named Desire* occurred in the very year of the founding in New York of the Actors Studio. Two months before the debut of *Streetcar,* the Studio was established as a gathering place for actors. It was founded by four people: Bobby Lewis,

Cheryl Crawford, Anna Sokolow, and Elia Kazan, who was the director of *Streetcar* and who had in the same year made a movie, *Gentleman's Agreement,* that would win the Oscar for Best Picture. Soon after the foundation, Lee Strasberg joined the Studio to become its teacher and its most authoritative figure.

There are those who regard the Actors Studio as a Church (and it has had illustrious members as well as a strange, long-running television show ready to showcase any actor), but the more devout we are in considering it, the less respect we have for the riddles in acting, and their comic undertone.[13]

In many respects, the Actors Studio was an offshoot of the Group Theatre, which had been established as a theatre collective in 1931, founded by Harold Clurman (a director of plays), Cheryl Crawford (a producer and director), and Lee Strasberg (a natural godfather). The Group believed in the value of art and theatre in a time of worldwide depression and political unrest. It was an organization of the Left that encouraged radical plays and had several members with allegiances to the Communist Party. It was their feeling that America needed and deserved an acting style of its own that was naturalistic, intimate, rooted in psychology, politically committed, and pledged to an independent formula for good work in the theatre. It was a group that included writers and directors as well as actors, and so it had Clurman and Strasberg, Clifford Odets and Irwin Shaw, and Luther and Stella Adler (brother and sister, actor and teacher). Elia Kazan joined the Group as a young actor and all-purpose assistant.

The notion of an American way of acting presupposed that the theatre had been unduly dominated by English acting and

English plays, and that the English style was grand but hollow or "mannered." In part that was directed at young stars, like Olivier and Gielgud, but it was strengthened by an American sense of inferiority towards the grand manner and stagey eloquence of British theatre, and its influence on the movies. Hollywood in the thirties was a welcoming place for the English voice—Ronald Colman, Cary Grant, Charles Laughton, David Niven, Basil Rathbone, Douglas Fairbanks Jr., John Barrymore even (an actor trained in the English style), Claude Rains, Robert Donat, Leslie Howard, Clive Brook, George Arliss, Errol Flynn. Among actresses, there were many stars who were English, or non-American, or who often sounded English even if they had been born in America: Claudette Colbert, Irene Dunne, Olivia de Havilland and Joan Fontaine, Margaret Sullavan, Marlene Dietrich, Garbo, and Ingrid Bergman. In many parts of America, Bette Davis and Katharine Hepburn sounded English. Not least was Vivien Leigh, a voice from sophisticated London, who had won the most desirable role in America, Scarlett O'Hara. The South in *Gone With the Wind* had three of its four stars with British credentials.

So there was some resentment towards British acting, coupled with an assumption that English-trained actors preferred to turn up and do their work, without fuss or theory (though Laughton was a neurotic exception to that). But in the first two decades of sound movies, an authentic American character emerged in acting. It was far more natural than theoretical; it was laconic, inward, often silent, and it had an instinctive appreciation of the kind of underplaying that the camera enjoyed. Cagney, Tracy,

Gable, and Bogart were all in this line. But the most restrained and natural was Gary Cooper. In fact, Cooper had been educated in Britain, but he did not let that show. He sounded clipped, dry, Western, and shy about speaking. He was famous for doing very little in the eyes of people on his sets, who were then astounded by the eloquence of his work, moment by moment, on screen. As far as we know Cooper had never read Stanislavsky's *An Actor Prepares,* and he never attended a session at the Actors Studio, but he was the ideal expression of a hope for inward American acting that seemed manly, honest, and damn good.

Cooper has neither dated nor explained himself. He made plenty of poor pictures, and he was not the sort of leader in the business who determined the parts he would play. He was a contract player who did as he was told. Even his best contemporaries look a little dated now. Cagney could be an overdrawn pastiche of himself. Gable liked to seem overconfident. Bogart was too protected by his nasty edge. Tracy is often grumpy and overly secure. I don't offer those comments aggressively. Those four are great movie actors still. But Cooper is mysterious and intact. He has a being that goes on way beyond his appearance or presence. He is still captivating, and tragic, though I suspect he could never have explained what he was doing. He was not an idiot. He had assessed the camera. But how it got at secret aspects of the soul—that is uncanny. James Stewart (so good) can look studied and even hammy. But Cooper and Cary Grant are matchless. They never did the one thing that tempts movie stars—playing themselves. It's as if they were too unsure of a self to go to.

I describe Cooper in this way because he was exactly what the Actors Studio wanted, while being as far beyond their grasp as he was deaf to their theories. Their stress on the teaching of Stanislavsky and other Russian writers, their search for sense memory and the actor's overlap with the psychology of a role are all essential to the Method and its era. It was in the 1940s that psychoanalysis began to be a cottage industry in Los Angeles, and it is still the most common and profitable acting school there has ever been. For the Group Theater, the Russian associations were a credential worth having. So many of their plays were direct (and blunt) social statements—like Clifford Odets's *Waiting for Lefty*, which premiered in 1935 and concerned a strike among cabdrivers, with the audience gathered like the crowd at union meetings. One of those strike leaders was played by Elia Kazan.

Kazan had wanted to be an actor and had to hear from others (notably from Lee Strasberg, a scold and aggressor) that he was not good enough, or good-looking enough, to play leads. So the role of the rejected actor became vital to Kazan's imagination, and it lurks beneath the resonant self-pity of some of the best modern American acting. Kazan believed he was giving it a radical, or insurrectionary thrust. But he was also digging back into the poetic reticence of Gary Cooper. *Waiting for Lefty* was a blatant trick of stagecraft, but Kazan lusted after the withdrawn intimacy of the movie camera. So the Method was always a map to Hollywood and film's allegation that we are spying on the actors' open wounds.

Just listen to Kazan, years later, in *A Life*, treasuring the moment of *Lefty* and seeing himself as a character he could play:

I was on the right path. *Lefty* had proved that. I carried the roar of the audience's approval in my ears.

As for the theatre? My future? The Group had reassured me now. I was one of the leaders now. I could keep my head up, rabbit's foot and all—yes, the Proletariat Thunderbolt! I could walk with the best. I knew the secret. I had the right technique. I'd proved my talent—as an actor and as a theatre person. I wasn't someone to be bawled out publicly for fucking up a goddamn misplanned earthquake. Look at me now, Lee! I am admired, respected, needed, acclaimed! I felt the special gaiety only confident people can enjoy. I was a man who'd stood central in a glorious, historic theatre event.

All this—however foolish it may sound now—made me into another person. I felt reborn, or born for the first time. The days of pain were over. I was an honored leader of the only good class, the working class, and the only real theatre, the Group. And they—the workers and the theatre—were united; they saw things together. I was finally, on top, every way. My dreams, the total dreams, had come true. For the first time in my memory, I was thrilled to be alive. I was everything I wanted to be.[14]

How can anyone be that jubilant without being a self-dramatist? But if so, must he be prepared to sink, too? To be an actor is to admit to the possibility of bipolarity: it is akin to being in work or not, having a role or a life, or waiting. Still, in 1935, at twenty-six, all seemed perfect for Kazan—except that he did not notice that *Waiting for Lefty* was a mediocre play, as threadbare and hollow as it was punchy. But actors do not always read plays, not the whole thing. They like their bit.

In Kazan's *A Life,* he describes a moment from a class given by Lee Strasberg to some young players in the Group Theatre. This was about 1932. Two actresses had played a scene for Strasberg.

When it ended, he said nothing. And still nothing. The silence persisted and the two young actresses became increasingly nervous. They asked what the master had thought. He turned away from them, in disdain. They broke into tears. Then he pounced. "Do you feel very insecure now?" he asked them. "Oh, yes!" they cried. "More than you did when you played the scene?" he demanded. "Oh, yes!" they agreed. But how could that be, Strasberg concluded, when you were supposed to be playing two very insecure young women?[15] (In just over forty years, he would play master mobster and polite intimidator Hyman Roth in *The Godfather Part II*.)

It is a devilish piece of education, and no one took it in more than Kazan. Whether it is true to the theories of Konstantin Stanislavsky on sense memory or to the potential authoritarian in Strasberg and Kazan is a matter of debate. But the point is sound and enlightening: there are states of being and experience that need to be real, and not just artful and polite pretense. The actor needs to possess the experience of the character and then reveal it to the audience. But must he be possessed by it? Should Strasberg have been as real and cold a killer as Roth?

Kazan had been too young at the time, but the event that lay behind Strasberg's teaching was the visit to America of the Moscow Arts Theatre in 1922–23. The Moscow Arts had been founded by Konstantin Stanislavsky and Vladimir Nemirovich-Danchenko in 1898, and it had then become a state institution. It believed in a standing company of actors that lived and rehearsed together, for years sometimes, and who created an ensemble style in which there were no obvious stars. Stanislavsky, a director as well as a teacher, believed in psychological exploration in which the actor would find memories from his own life that enriched the experience of his character.[16] Such feelings were not simply Russian, or treated without criticism in Russia. In his theatre novel *Black Snow,* Mikhail Bulgakov mocks a figure like Stanislavsky and his theories. Much later, in his book *The Fervent Years,* Harold Clurman said that the Method "should never have been made a subject of conversation, a matter of publicity or Sunday articles, for it does not concern the audience."[17]

The Moscow players' tour of America happened to coincide with Barrymore's *Hamlet.* Always an ensemble, the Russians went as a group to see a matinee and they were staggered. One actress asked Barrymore, "Do you really do this eight times a week?" Stanislavsky himself set Barrymore a test: there was a pin hidden in the next room—go find it. He then observed Barrymore make the search—successfully—like Sherlock Holmes, with deeply felt naturalism. Stanislavsky offered to hire him. But the Russian actress had guessed correctly, too. After a dozen performances of Hamlet, Barrymore grew bored and started to improvise.[18]

Clurman and Cheryl Crawford visited Moscow in 1935 and eagerly questioned the elderly Stanislavsky (he would die in 1938). Something was bound to alter acting, for the broad style of stage acting could seem bogus and tedious, and it had been exposed by motion pictures. We may feel now that much silent screen acting was unduly signaled, struggling against the mute condition. But the audience had been stunned and moved by the new intimacy of the medium. That came in the chance to observe faces closely in moments of feeling. The close-up altered acting far more than Stanislavsky or Strasberg. Yet there are astonishing performances in silent cinema: Lillian Gish in many films, but especially in *Broken Blossoms* and *The Wind;* Rene Falconetti in Carl Dreyer's *The Passion of Joan of Arc;* Louise Brooks in *Pandora's Box;* Buster Keaton in nearly everything he ever did; Rudolph Valentino in a glance; Lon Chaney in so many of his grand guignol masterpieces. And even Gary Cooper for a few moments in *The Winning of Barbara Worth.*

No one in theatre had seen faces before in this way. So acting was a more fully physical thing. But the crudest cinema offered the chance that we might observe being. Theatrical historians have also noted that in the first decades of the twentieth century stage lighting increased in power and subtlety so that the masklike makeup of the Victorian era was no longer necessary. Again, the movies played their part in that, for glaring makeup only detracts from a sense of reality when photographed.

The Moscow Arts Theatre had another impact that enhanced their appearance in America in 1922–23. Anton Chekhov's *The Seagull* was produced in Saint Petersburg in 1896, and laughed off the stage because its stress on mood and inner realism was thought impossibly gloomy and boring. But the leaders of the Moscow Arts had been so impressed with the play and were so determined to revive Chekhov's crushed spirits that they remounted *The Seagull* for 1898, with Stanislavsky directing. In the next few years, Chekhov became associated with the Moscow Arts and with Stanislavsky—*Uncle Vanya, The Three Sisters,* and *The Cherry Orchard* were all done there before the playwright's death in 1904.

Some Chekhov had been staged in America. But the translations were inept or the style seemed awkward. It is inexplicable now—did the Great War have to intervene?—but the comic melancholy in Chekhov had not quite registered yet. When the Moscow Arts toured in 1922–23, the plays of Chekhov were their featured material, and the principle was renewed that a great theatre company can reveal itself the best in good plays.

Chekhov and Stanislavsky had worked together, and somehow their gentle, wistful view of hopelessly adrift upper-middle-class lives had survived the Revolution's assault on bourgeois ways without rebuke or censorship. Was it simply that Chekhov was so sublime, or that the creative aspirations of the company were so well served by his stagecraft and his language?

The Group Theatre had no better playwright than Clifford Odets—and it was not inclined to attempt the classics, as if that would have been a betrayal of American originality. But the pioneering of American prose fiction in the twenties and early thirties (Hemingway, Fitzgerald, Faulkner, Dreiser, Cather, West) was not matched in the theatre. Odets was inconsistent, and he finally settled for an old-fashioned hit, with *Golden Boy,* about a young man torn between being a boxer and a violinist, that found its proper destiny in an effective but softened movie melodrama —that's where Barbara Stanwyck encountered the young William Holden. So the Group Theatre offerings competed none too successfully with the varied but unreliable works of Eugene O'Neill, the comedies of writers as deft as Phillip Barry, Moss Hart, and George Kaufman, and the piercing if shallow mock epic theatre of the Mercury, led by Orson Welles. Harold Clurman was one of the first to note that Welles's Mercury drew attention but never caused offense, and had "a fundamental lack of seriousness." Welles reached gravity only in his movies.[19]

The many ideas within the Group Theatre had not yet made a significant change in American acting—nothing compared to the miracle of technological recessiveness instigated by the movies. So, in the early 1940s, when it was enough to look at faces and their altered minds, American acting was Henry Fonda as Tom Joad in *The Grapes of Wrath,* Gary Cooper in *Meet John Doe* or *The Pride of the Yankees,* Mickey Rooney and Judy Garland putting on a show, and even Orson Welles as *Citizen Kane.* Most people had noticed that film more than its performances. But for those with eyes and ears prepared to attend, Welles had delivered a character who was less insincere than incapable of believing in sincerity. His Kane was a remarkable, innovative, and nearly desperate portrait of a chronic actor.

Not many actors went to war, least of all those—like John Wayne, Errol Flynn, and Cooper—who played so many wartime heroes. Elia Kazan, thirty-three in 1942, was designated 3-A (deferred because of hardship to wife and children). He chose to think it was probably because the draft board knew of his brief membership in the Communist Party—already, he saw that adventure as his "rosebud." Marlon Brando, eighteen in 1942, and soon to be the epitome of a new masculinity, plus a revolutionary if not heroic actor, was 4-F because of a bad knee. So they spent a lot of the war in New York. It was never planned, or organized; they did not know each other yet, but they were made to be collaborators. Still, if they hadn't met on a small thing called *Truckline Café*, in 1946, who knows how different the world would be?[20]

Truckline Cafe was a disaster. One critic called it the worst play he had ever seen, and it closed after ten performances. It was a play by Maxwell Anderson about the stresses on men returning from the war. The team that put it on was Harold Clurman as director and Elia Kazan as producer. There was one scene in the play where a disturbed ex-soldier, Sage, staggers in from the ocean and confesses that he has killed his adulterous wife. The part was given by Clurman to Marlon Brando, who had played in *I Remember Mama* in 1944. He was an odd twenty-two-year-old, a very ambitious actor who was famously unconvincing in or unready for auditions, and who could be alarmingly hesitant or withdrawn in rehearsals. But he was very handsome; he had a riotous sexual life; and there was an unmistakable magnetism and potency to him. In casting Brando, Clurman had listened to his ex-wife, Stella Adler (they had divorced in 1943), who had made Brando her protégé and who was confident that he had inner powers just waiting to burst out. Marlon and Stella were close, and it is likely that they had had a sexual relationship (even as Marlon romanced her daughter, Ellen).

The *Truckline* rehearsals did not go well. Clurman was soon shouting at Brando that he could not be heard: he spoke too softly; he turned away from characters and the audience; he was too easily drawn to using the sighs and groans of uncertainty instead of the text. It was as if he couldn't find his role yet in a play that seemed foggy. Kazan was of the same opinion, though coming at it from a different direction. He knew the play was going to fail:

> Despite—or along with—my disappointment, I took a perverse pleasure in the failure of the performance. That's not a pretty confession, but it's true. I couldn't talk like Harold, but I sure as hell would have done something about that playscript. I'd have kept after the author until he improved his play. I wouldn't have sat by, being brilliant and adored, while the play failed. I might even have interfered with the rights of the playwright given him by the Dramatists Guild and "fussed" with the text. Harold had said, when I'd indicated my impatience with the meager extent of Max's rewriting, "That's the play. You can't do anything about it. It will succeed or fail, but that's it." This fatalism I found intolerable.[21]

Kazan was already fascinated by a lesson he had taken from Strasberg, which in turn had been learned from Vsevolod Meyerhold: "The actor no longer occupies the leading place upon the stage. The director will determine all life there."[22] The ambition to direct, and the subsequent realization that the director should be a vital leader, was growing in Kazan: he had directed *The Skin of Our Teeth* on Broadway in 1942, and the next year he went to Hollywood to make his first movie, *A Tree Grows in Brooklyn.*

The battle between Clurman and Brando, or the struggle to get the actor to harness and deliver his power, was not something from which Kazan could stay an outsider. In later years, Kazan would be known for private, whispered conferences with actors in which he gave them the clue and they thrived on his wisdom. It was Kazan who told Brando that he should undertake violent exercises before Sage's entrance so that he would be truly breathless, and it was Kazan who threw a bucket of water on the actor so that Sage would seem like someone who had just emerged from the sea. Then in the scene where Sage confessed the murder to his waitress, he got Brando to beat on the table with his fists so that crockery jumped and broke. It was an odd harbinger of Stanley Kowalski in *A Streetcar Named Desire*.

The play was a lost venture, but Brando's scenes were thought astonishing. He stopped the show. Many in the company felt sure they were seeing a great force in the making. He was voted Most Promising Newcomer for 1946. According to another actor in the play, Richard Waring, Brando even added a pause and changed a couple of lines to ensure that he would get a burst of applause at his exit. Why not? What is a young actor doing in the professional theatre but trying to get ahead? And sometimes that means teaching the audience to respect your act. I directed a play once in which an actress was doing a superb job. But she was shy, or reticent, and maybe fundamentally uneasy over acting. At the end of the show, she got great applause. But I knew she deserved a standing ovation, and I believed that the audience wanted to give it to her. But she resisted her own glory. She was casual, offhand, even a little disdainful. So I taught her to be in awe of the audience and then touched by their kindness. It was a matter of timing and flattery. She got the standing ovation, but I think she always believed I had pulled a dishonest trick. She gave up acting after a while—but so did Marlon Brando.

Truckline Café opened and closed in March 1946. By then, Tennessee Williams was writing a play that would be called *The Poker Night* before it found its eventual identity as *A Streetcar*

Named Desire. Set in New Orleans, the play concerns a young married couple, Stanley Kowalski and Stella DuBois. Stella seldom bears her family name in the play, but the ethnic collision is essential, and Williams stresses how unalike they are at the outset. This is a union of the Old South, with European associations, and Master Sergeant Kowalski of the Engineers' Corps who fought at Salerno. Call him a Polack and he'll tell you he's one hundred per cent American. He relishes reminding Stella that she found him "common," yet full of sexual energy, and he has to match the horrified view of Stella's older sister, Blanche, when she comes to visit:

> He acts like an animal, has an animal's habits! Eats like one, moves like one, talks like one! There's even something—sub-human—something not quite to the stage of humanity yet! Yes, something—ape-like about him, like one of those pictures I've seen in—anthropological studies! Thousands and thousands of years have passed him right by, and there he is—Stanley Kowalski—survivor of the stone age! Bearing the raw meat home from the kill in the jungle![23]

So here we are with America the refined and the raw. Blanche and Stella are of the South, and its Belle Reve plantation. But the play never knows where Stanley has come from. The stage directions say he is twenty-eight to thirty, old enough to have fought through the war. And the action emphasizes his physicality: he sweats when he bowls; he likes to take off his wet shirt; and in a crisis he clears the table the old-fashioned, stone age way: he throws the chinaware on the floor. When you read the play there is no doubt but that it is Blanche's story: she has so many more lines and all the heartbreak scenes. She is the most sensitive person in the play. She will end stripped of lies and illusion, raped and taken away to an asylum. It reads like her tragedy, but it plays as something far subtler.

The rights to produce the play were bought by Irene Selznick, a Hollywood person, the daughter of Louis B. Mayer and the wife to David O. Selznick, though they had separated.[24] She wanted Joshua Logan to direct, but she accepted Kazan on Williams's urging, and then Kazan had tried to get her fired. The first thought for Stanley was the Hollywood actor John Garfield, who had once worked with the Group Theatre and created the role of Ralph in Odets's *Awake and Sing* (1935). By 1947, when *Streetcar* opened, Garfield was thirty-four; he was Jewish and he had the air of the working class about him. The part could have been his, but he would do it only if the role were enlarged and made equal to Blanche, and if he got a better deal fit for a movie star. Other actors were considered—Burt Lancaster, who was also thirty-four. Kazan insisted on Brando, who would be twenty-three in 1947, barely old enough to have had Stanley's military career and too close to beautiful to sustain the idea of Stone Age man.

Kazan promoted this casting; it was his vision or his guess, but it was his manoeuver, too. He located Brando, carousing in New York—not the easiest man to find—gave him $20 in cash, and told him to go and see Tennessee Williams in Provincetown. Brando made the trip, at his own pace: "take a moment" was one of Lee Strasberg's key policies for an actor facing an intense moment. So Brando missed his first loose appointment with Williams. But a day or two later he emerged as a providential fixer.

The lavatory was blocked in the Provincetown house and Brando played a plumber. He went down on his knees and with his bare hands he freed the blockage. Williams was enchanted with the good-looking savior. He asked Brando to read from the play. Within days, Williams was writing to his agent, Audrey Wood:

> I can't tell you what a relief it is that we have found such a God-sent Stanley in the person of Brando. It had not occurred to me before why an excellent value would come through casting a very young actor in this part. It humanizes the character of Stanley in that it becomes the brutality or callousness of youth rather than a vicious older man. I don't want to focus guilt or blame particularly on any one character but to have it a tragedy of misunderstanding and insensitivity to others. A new value came out of Brando's reading which was by far the best reading I have ever heard. He seemed to have already created a dimensional character, of the sort that the war has produced among young veterans. This is a value beyond anything that Garfield could have contributed, and in addition to his gifts as an actor he has great physical appeal and sensuality, at least as much as Burt Lancaster.[25]

There's no reason to call this process "rewriting," but in casting and rehearsal, an alert writer can discover the inner world of his or her play. The interaction may be unconscious (perhaps it is best that way), but it cannot and should not be avoided. In important ways, Brando was "wrong" for Stanley. It didn't matter, and it did focus author and director in a remarkable and beneficial way. Kazan said later that he had been wary of the play. He never quite said why, and he stressed that he and Williams became friends. Still, Williams was as openly gay as 1947 permitted, and Kazan was resolutely not gay. Instead, he was a chronic womanizer. He was also a director who needed to identify with his material. By the time he became a confirmed movie director, this was his strength. It was an attitude learned from Strasberg's theories, but it was Kazan's need, too.

The play was about Blanche—anyone could see that. In the years since, *Streetcar* has been so identified: Uta Hagen, Blythe Danner, Claire Bloom, Ann-Margret (on TV), Jessica Lange, Renee Fleming (in the opera), Rachel Weisz, Cate Blanchett, Gillian Anderson. (It's hard to recall their Stanleys.) In fact, the touring production of 1948, with Uta Hagen and Anthony Quinn, was directed by Harold Clurman instead of Kazan, and Clurman pointedly shifted attention back to Blanche. But if the play was to succeed at the deepest level in December 1947, then it had to be about Kazan, too. That meant the director was bound to identify with Stanley as a dark, volatile, sexual outlaw blowing away the fuss and pretension of a dishonest fantasist.

No one knows how far Williams grasped this at the time, but hindsight commentary has seen the "date" between Stanley and Blanche as a gay metaphor in which the refined man meets rough trade. Such a reading was hardly viable in 1947 in a hit play on Broadway. But the effectiveness of the work matches the date between Kazan and Williams as much as that between the two characters in the play. Kazan would say that he was relieved and persuaded to sign on when Williams told him that Stanley was not to be a brute, a villain, and a rapist (and surely those things exist in the text), but a truculent young war veteran threatened in his own home and fearing that his wife, Stella, may reject her old attraction to commonness and raw meat under the influence of Blanche.

So Kazan placed himself on Stanley's side. He became like an older brother to Brando and he encouraged the actor to be as forthright and erotic as possible. Whenever Stanley was on stage, it should be clear that he was the power in the household. Just to cement and feel for that bond, Kazan had a love affair with Kim Hunter, the actress he had cast as Stella.

As for Blanche, there were the usual arguments. Apparently, Williams had thought of Tallulah Bankhead (from Alabama). Another early idea had been to cast Margaret Sullavan in the part. Here was a movie actress as well as a stage player, thirty-eight in 1947, very attractive, with a great fragile voice. Moreover, she had been born in Virginia. But when she did a reading, observers said she was like a woman carrying a tennis racket—in other words, she introduced a misleading atmosphere of drawing room comedy. She seemed to be out of touch with the desires that lie behind Blanche's ladylike act. Instead, the role went to Jessica Tandy, who was English and also thirty-eight. She had appeared on the London stage, as Ophelia to John Gielgud's Hamlet and as the French princess to Olivier's Henry V. Before that she had had one Broadway job, in *The Matriarch* (1930). She had been married to an English actor, Jack Hawkins, and after that to a Canadian actor, Hume Cronyn. She had appeared in a few movies by 1947, but she had not had a recent stage role in America.

Tandy was good-looking and ladylike, and she could do the southern accent, but she was not quite sexually vibrant. She won the Tony as Blanche (sharing it with Judith Anderson and Katharine Cornell), and she was playing the lead in a sensational stage event. She did not let the play down. There are photographs of her with Brando's Stanley in which she seems like a wounded bird with him as the hunter. No one who saw the play ever complained. But Brando thought she was miscast—he thought the same about himself—and Kazan described a rehearsal period in which he was urged on by Hume Cronyn to dig deeper into Tandy, to make her better and more elemental. Kazan saw that there was a tendency for Tandy to hold to her way of doing things which only drew attention to the dangerous spontaneity of Brando's Stanley:

> Hers seemed to be a performance; Marlon was living on stage. Jessie had every moment worked out, carefully, with sensitivity and intelligence, and it was all coming together, just as Williams and I had expected and wanted. Marlon, working "from the inside," rode his emotion wherever it took him; his performance was full of surprises and exceeded what Williams and I had expected. A performance miracle was in the making. What was there to do but be grateful?[26]

For those there on the first night of *Streetcar* or during the first run, Brando was the center of attention. But that was not fair to the play they were playing, and it is far from the historical record. *A Streetcar Named Desire* is established as one of our great plays and in the years since it premiered, our sexual nature has been treated with so much more candor that it's possible to see both overt action and dream metaphor in the play. But in 1947, the production was a vivid example of the contrast or conflict between American and English acting.

That was a loaded and inaccurate interpretation. Tandy had lived for years in America. Brando would say later that he was never an Actors Studio kind of guy. He owed far more to Stella Adler than to Lee Strasberg (a man he never liked). So a great deal sprang from the bond between Brando and Kazan, the way they fed off each other, and to the first notable liberation of the instinctive behavior in Brando, the way he could be brutal and gentle, violent and thoughtful, at the same time. He was a great actor far more than he was a Method actor. And his presence was a close run thing. He had decided he was wrong for the part—as I said, he was never convinced by it, largely because he was far gentler and more thoughtful than Stanley. He had telephoned Kazan to say "no." But the line was busy. He didn't reach Kazan until a few hours later, and by then his mood had shifted or weakened—he ended up saying he would do it. So it could have been . . . Burt Lancaster, Anthony Quinn, or Kirk Douglas? Would that have ruined the effect, or simply led it in a different direction? We don't have to decide, but casting is the arbitrary but inescapable wind that blows every sail along. It defies the theory that anyone is ever "right" for a part. The real action may be in overcoming the wrongness.

A few years later, the movie of *Streetcar* was taken up at Warner Brothers. Kazan began by saying he wanted to be loyal to "his" stage cast. Then he said the studio required a star for Blanche. Was it them, or was it Kazan? He felt badly towards Jessica Tandy, yet he sold her out and admitted later that he believed he needed a change, "a high-voltage shock to get my motor going." The new decision was novelettish: once again the role of the Belle Reve dreamer was given to an English woman, but now it was Vivien Leigh. After all, she had played southern before. And she had been a very distressed Blanche in London as directed by the husband who admitted that he neither liked nor understood the play. However, imagine the fresh enthusiasm Olivier might have found in himself if *he* had been asked to play Stanley. Not good casting?

A Moment Later

Scene 1 Imagine the transparent ribbon of film rushing through the projector. Washed clean of signs and pictures, it produces a flickering reflected light from the screen. From the loudspeakers we hear only the noise of the amplifier and the faint crackle of dust particles travelling through the playback head.

I f it seems ridiculous to think of Olivier rivaling Brando as
Stanley Kowalski, then we are entering the conundrum of
casting. No one would have charged that Olivier *was* Stanley, or came close to him. But Brando had similar reservations
about himself. Olivier did play Tennessee Williams: he was Big
Daddy in a British television version of *Cat on a Hot Tin Roof*,
with Natalie Wood as Maggie and Robert Wagner as Brick. All
of that left something to be desired, and Olivier was anxious that
Maureen Stapleton (his Big Momma) give him dialect lessons.
But if that was mediocre, Olivier's Hurstwood in the William
Wyler film of *Carrie* (from Dreiser's novel), elegant and forlorn,
acting to conceal his desperation from himself, is one of the best
things he ever did. It is unquestionably American, just as his
Szell (the Nazi dentist) in *Marathon Man* is plausibly if melo-
dramatically German, just as his Mahdi in *Khartoum* is a bold
gesture towards being Arabic, and just as the Moor of Venice was
hailed as one of his greatest successes in *Othello*.

It was possible for Olivier skeptics to sigh over his black face,
his Ali Baba's cavern of new voices, and the great collection
of noses from which, notoriously, he began many of his roles.
Those attributes seem to expose Olivier the pretender, the helpless devotee of makeup and mock-up, the actor who could never

resist any challenge to his versatility. In the first great fame of the Method—in the years after *Streetcar* until about the end of the 1950s—it was possible for Strasbergians to make an Olivier seem not just mercurial or versatile but ungrounded, or uninterested in substance. So it was the alleged realism, the emotional actuality and the integrity, of Brando's Stanley and then his Terry Malloy in *On the Waterfront* that became banners for the Actors Studio.

But then see what happened with Brando: he was a paraplegic in *The Men;* he was a biker rebel in *The Wild One;* he was a Mexican in *Viva Zapata!;* he was a punch-drunk boxer in *On the Waterfront;* he was Olivier-like as Marc Antony in *Julius Caesar;* he was Napoleon in *Désirée;* he sang and danced as Sky Masterson in *Guys and Dolls;* he was a comic Okinawan in *Teahouse of the August Moon* and a blond German officer in *The Young Lions*—where, truth be told, his accent was not as credible as Olivier's in *Marathon Man.* Brando had no paralysis: he does not really seem like a stricken man in *The Men;* he looks like a hero pretending to be an invalid. He studied paraplegia; he went to stay in a veterans' hospital; he did all the research he could to understand the experience of war's victims. He was not French or Okinawan or German or Mexican. In all those roles he used makeup—noses sometimes; he altered his hair and he found a new voice. And he seemed entertained by the idea of taking on ever-wilder challenges, even if sometimes—as in *Désirée*—you can see and feel his dismay over the poor scripts and note the first signs of his famous inwardness turning towards disillusion and contempt. If there is a vital difference between Brando and Olivier, it is in the fact that Olivier never yielded to that contempt, to its eventual self-loathing, or to a fatigue with pretending.

A comparison with James Dean is illuminating. Dean was only a few years younger than Brando, and he became a new and supplanting discovery in Kazan's career—*East of Eden* came right after *On the Waterfront*. Dean was plainly inspired by Brando, which is not to detract from the younger man's own brilliance or pathos. But in what proved to be his last film, *Giant,* Dean faced a special challenge. He played the young Jett Rink to perfection—a moody, insecure ranch hand, envious, romantic, spiteful, yearning, cunning, yet oddly soulless. But then in the passage of time that made two parts of that labored film, Dean had to age thirty years and become Rink the tycoon, gray-haired, alcoholic, self-pitying, morose, still nasty and utterly soulless. He made a brave effort at it, though we have chosen to remember the Dean who played his own age. But it was a masquerade of middle age that exposed Dean's limits as a technical actor and as someone struggling to know more about life.

In 1972, when he was forty-eight, Brando put padding in his mouth, gray in his hair; he found a groaning whisper, and his act of pretending acquired the age of a man who was meant to be in his mid-sixties. Yes, Brando was older than Dean had been, but Vito Corleone in *The Godfather* is a more convincing or natural portrait of resolute age and the conflict between immigrant ambition and enforced wickedness in a man. We can regard that as a matter of technique, but Brando was the more experienced pretender of the two, and more aware that the actor needed to leave a hidden area, more secret than ingratiating or self-pitying.

There is a great gap between playing with a naked heart and one that is guarded or secret—but most people in life *are* guarded. In constructing a part, Brando and others (Philip Seymour Hoffman is another) appreciate those areas and possibilities left out of sight. In watching actors we want to see the whole person, but in life we know there are things we never quite grasp about people who are very close to us. In that context, Stella Adler (the chief influence on Brando's method) had gone to study with Stanislavsky in Paris in the late 1930s. The old man told her that his ideas had evolved: he was inclined by then to believe less in sense memory and the reality of a character existing in the actor than in imagination and pretending.

Brando was never a leader of gangsters or a murderer; he was not Sicilian. He had been no closer to his great roles (or his foolish ones) than Olivier could ever claim. As great actors they were very alike in that their own reality had succumbed in so many ways to the career of pretending. Recall the casting process, and you can feel the truth of this: Brando was not obvious casting as Vito, and the studio, Paramount, had many reservations because he had made wayward films in the sixties. He was more difficult to handle, but less sure of himself. There were other people being talked about as Vito: Frank Sinatra, Robert Mitchum, Ernest Borgnine. You may be smiling at this list—Sinatra as Vito Corleone? But many people felt it was ridiculous in 1952 that he might be cast as the rebellious soldier, Maggio, in *From Here to Eternity.* That role changed his life and the way we thought of him. It won him an Oscar and it may have provided an assurance that made him a greater or more mature singer.

(Moreover, he may have possessed useful, sidelong experience in those family matters.) So casting urges caution on the onlooker, and in this case it may call to mind that Francis Coppola, the director of *The Godfather,* was himself torn between two actors for Vito—Marlon Brando and Laurence Olivier.

From what you've seen of Olivier and what you know of him, is it possible that the sixty-five-year-old English actor could have done Don Vito? Well, surely he could not have been Brando's Vito; but that does not consider his own man—colder, weaker, more devious, less adored by Caan, Duvall, and Pacino than regarded from a respectful distance? Surely, many sons fear their father and are daunted by him? Olivier was adept at playing fragile yet tough old men in whom softness and cruelty were mixed. In 1972, on stage and in a TV film, he played James Tyrone, that shabby ex-actor, sentimental but mean, selfish yet ruined by the plight of his family, in *Long Day's Journey into Night.* Tyrone was an American actor, based on the figure of Eugene O'Neill's own father. Everyone who saw Olivier's Tyrone was convinced and moved by every detail. I cannot believe that, if forced to be Don Vito, if given an offer he couldn't refuse, Olivier would not have found stealth, irony, fondness, malice, and great danger in the man. This is not to say he would have been "better" than Brando. But wouldn't you like to see Olivier's Vito Corleone as much as you might hope to see Brando's Hamlet or his James Tyrone? But here's another point: could Brando have summoned the necessary self-loathing for Tyrone?

Casting is a professional process and an endless prospect for the imagination. The process is based on the ability to know the range of people who are available and might be suitable, and to have the ear of the film's director or producer so that you know the way they are thinking. Casting is also an imprint of box office. Some actors ensure a green light for a project through their presence. There had been a time when Brando was such a star—with an Oscar, reputation, and several reasonable hits—that any project came to life if he said he would do it. That's when he made his bad films. No experience seems to have done more to sap his eagerness and faith than the way his eminence led to unsatisfying work: *The Fugitive Kind, One-Eyed Jacks, Mutiny on the Bounty, The Ugly American, Bedtime Story, Morituri, The Chase, The Appaloosa, A Countess from Hong Kong, Reflections in a Golden Eye, Candy, The Night of the Following Day, Burn!, The Nightcomers.*

There are films in that list you have forgotten or never heard of. It is not a worthless series—*Burn!* (directed by Gillo Pontecorvo in Latin America) is a fascinating political adventure, *Reflections in a Golden Eye* (by John Huston, with Brando as a gay military officer) was years ahead of its time, *The Chase* (by Arthur Penn, with Brando sheriff of a corrupt and violent Texas town) is sometimes close to a major film. But several of those movies are very bad. Most reports say Brando's mercenary intransigence helped destroy *Mutiny on the Bounty,* as he spent more time and energy reveling in Tahiti and its people. *One-Eyed Jacks,* the film he directed, went on so long and in such confusion that Brando eventually quit the editing of his own work and left others to finish it. He would never try to direct again. So many of the films he made on a whim and a caprice, and because his name swayed the decision. But Brando became disenchanted in the process. Olivier never stopped acting. Even when he was probably too ill to carry a large part, he did cameos of invalidism.

Casting is more useful in the smaller roles. *The Godfather* got Brando; but the effectiveness of the casting on that film is in the detail, and what are sometimes called the supporting roles. This is not just Al Pacino, James Caan, Robert Duvall, and Diane Keaton—and all those roles were in fierce competition, so that the picture might have been Warren Beatty, Anthony Perkins, Bruce Dern, and Mia Farrow. But the casting work led by Fred Roos also meant Abe Vigoda as Tessio, Sterling Hayden as Mc-Cluskey, Al Lettieri as Sollozzo, Talia Shire as Connie, Richard Conte as Barzini—all the way to Gabrielle Torrei as Enzo the baker, Simoneta Stefanelli as Apollonia, the Sicilian bride, John Marley as Jack Woltz the Hollywood producer who wakes with a horse's head in his bed. They even had to find the right horse. And don't forget John Cazale as Fredo, who makes *Part II* and stands up for human weakness as a natural thing not to be intimidated by cruel strength.

There is a care over casting in most Coppola films that builds their texture and their pleasure. The same density is there in many films of John Ford, Frank Capra, Howard Hawks, Jean Renoir, Martin Scorsese, and a range of other directors. A lot of those actors become parts of the director's creative family—so Walter Brennan worked six times with Hawks, Ward Bond made fourteen films for John Ford, and Regis Toomey did one for Frank Capra. Only one? That doesn't sound like much, yet Toomey's honest guy in *Meet John Doe* is in many ways the sentimental heart of Capra-ism. And I mention Toomey for another reason, that of persistence: he made pictures and television from 1929 to 1982, and he accumulated 266 credits, including single entries for television series where he would have been in several episodes. You can get the feeling that Regis Toomey was in everything.

And I can't remember when he wasn't swell. Does that mean that he was a good actor? Were Brennan and Bond good actors? Well, they were regular delights, enormously skilled in the formulaic genres of American pictures. Could Brennan have played Lear? Could Bond have done Macbeth? Was there an Uncle Vanya in Regis Toomey? In all likelihood these pros hardly bothered to consider such questions. You could say that they played themselves, that casting people or directors shouted out, "I'm going to need a Walter Brennan type!" It followed that a director on set could sigh with relief because, while the actress was being so difficult that she required a lot of attention, he had Regis Toomey on this next scene—and Toomey didn't need directing. He looked at the script. He knew the kind of film it was. He saw the wardrobe they had for him. And he may have been smart enough to survey the lighting and the lens so that he foresaw the shot he was in. Then he did it. Directing a film is such a pressure on time and nervous energy, that anyone who can just do it is gold. That's why those people keep getting cast, so long as they look like themselves.

This is close to the common phrase, "straight from Central Casting." That institution exists still, but it is not as important as it was. Central Casting was where a picture went to fill its small parts. You spoke to Central Casting in code—you said you wanted this or that stereotype: a fading southern gentlewoman; a lean and hungry hobo; an English colonel; a beautiful blonde looking for her big break; or even a comic black maid. Film and folklore are filled with these rigidly defined types (or clichés). Maybe *you* could be described that way in the circle of your acquaintances. They might assess you in a sentence. You could protest that you're much richer than that type—you're unique, you're interesting, you're special; you are the center of your attention. But the world has you typed, the way advertising, politics, and your server know your demographic and your trends. And some types go a surprisingly long way. Every now and then America wants a cheery, friendly, honest guy who talks wry sense, cracks old jokes, and waves at the camera—get me Ronald Reagan. Of course, he had had good training and he was president of the Screen Actors Guild before any other presidency came his way.

Central Casting would supply actors who would be good for a scene, a couple of days' work, and a few lines. This is getting close to another category of players, and one that begins to show how easily the bright, accented world of types and cameos could lead into a Kafka anonymity. For there were extras. These were people who filled the background. If Bogart and Bacall were at a table at the end of *The Big Sleep* getting sexy, the film might need twenty other diners or waiters to make the restaurant feel in business. In the opening of François Truffaut's *Day for Night*, a street scene is being shot at the Victorine Studio in Nice. It involves a confrontation between characters played by Jean-Pierre Aumont and Jean-Pierre Leaud. But the scene has complex camera movements in which a dozen or so extras have to be ready to pass in the background to help us believe the scene is real. As the scene is shot several times, we see them doing their walk and then going back to their mark again for a fresh take. People worked their whole lives as extras, and their pay varied depending on whether they needed costume or wore their own clothes. The trick to being an extra was to be marginally vivid or interesting, without quite being noticed. Because if a director felt he recognized an extra he'd throw her out for overfamiliarity. Day after day, these people had to be themselves but invisible. You begin to see how stealthily acting overlaps with life.

Since life has come up again as a subject, we might as well face the most hideous change of all in acting. There was a time when you yearned for something and your parents told you, "You'll have to wait until you grow up." This seemed wise if tormenting advice. Your father and mother were older than you were, so somehow that gap had been arranged with mutual advantages: you were guided and they were energized in leadership. You may not have realized it at the time, but your existence perhaps made their lives bearable or explicable. They kept count of your height on the doorpost: pencil marks at every birthday, chipping with the dry paint, but testament to youth and growth. At a certain point that ragged staircase stops. There will be no one there to track the time when you begin to shrink or stoop. But the pencil marks may remain long after you have lost or sold the house, until some newcomers paint them over and start to record the upward mobility of their own children.

We move forward, one day, one year, after another. Life may have its doldrum passages, but then a storm comes along, and

126 *A Moment Later*

progress and motion are renewed. Thirty comes after twenty-nine, and so on.

There was a young actor. Everyone told him he was full of promise. He had done a few things on stage, A Messenger, Lucky in *Godot,* and the Porter in *Macbeth.* He applied himself to these parts with diligence and developing skill. He was admired. And then one day he was offered a movie, a thing he had been warned about, though no one had told him a tenth of the upheaval.

They had no title yet for the movie, and no script. There were many conflicting ideas about what it would be. But they knew they wanted this young actor for what they called "the lead."

"He is a happy young man. He has a sweet girlfriend. They are going to be married, though they have not yet become lovers. It is 1950, when such things happened, or did not happen.

"One night, he is in a driving accident on a country road. There is a great collision and he loses consciousness. Are you with us?

"The next thing he knows he is in a hospital bed, and he feels very strange, but he no longer has the power to describe his alteration. He has been in a coma for seven years. Do you see? Seven years!

"Well," they said, drawing in a deep breath. "Everything has changed. His girl despaired. She married another man. They have children. Our hero is very sad. In addition, he cannot walk, and he is bewildered by the aftermath of his coma. You can imagine. He feels he has no life.

"Then he discovers that sometimes, in just a simple touch or even an exchanged glance, he can picture the lives of others. And he has a gift of prescience. He can see disasters or mishaps that are coming. So he begins to fill his life by rescuing other people from their futures. Do you like it so far . . . ?"

The young actor does not know what not to like. He is being paid $1 for the film. It is spelled out in a contract that defines the installments of his fee in terms of "signature," "principal photography" and "opening." He can plan for the future. So he has no objections. He asks about the script and the storyline and he is told not to worry. Those things will be worked out "as time moves on."

"Monday," they say.

And on the Monday, he is filmed. It is an elaborate shot that takes all day in the cold in which he emerges from a house on a town street, hobbles over a road, and moves on to join a growing crowd that is gathering for an open-air political meeting. He asks about his character's state of mind and he is told that it is a long shot so his state of mind will not show. It is an action shot in which he should do the walk, but do it with a limp because, after all, his character is in a struggle to regain the ability to walk. They take the shot several times, with a tracking camera, and the young actor is pleased to be told he is a natural.

Tuesday, Wednesday pass and nothing more happens. But on Thursday, he is told about Friday. He is to enter an old house, go up the dark staircase and find a menacing old woman who asks what he is doing. He wonders why this house and this old woman, and he is told that his character has "seen" that the old woman's son is a killer, and he has come to the house to confront the killer. But the mother is there and he realizes that she knows *everything* and will try to kill *him*.

He should have trouble with the staircase—he can hardly walk. "Does this come before or after I cross the street and go to the meeting?" he wonders.

"Ah!" says the director. "I'm not sure—not sure yet. Just have a hard time with the stairs."

So he does his best and he works with the actress playing the old woman, and she is more alarming in life than in her part. She is drunk in life, but not in the film, and she seems serenely experienced at that impossible transition.

"Monday," they say, "next Monday. Nice scene. Your girlfriend."

He has not yet filmed anything with the girlfriend, though he has been led to believe that there will be a setup scene with her, before the accident ever occurred. But this next Monday's scene is later on, much later on. The girl comes to see him at his house, where he limps around and tries to forget his coma. She comes to the house because she believes they should at last make love—just the one time—so that its possibility is not forgotten. In this scene, she sits down beside him on a sofa, gazes at him in a mysterious way and starts to undress. The actress is very pleasant and everyone agrees that undressed she is even more pleasant. The young man has to embrace her and touch her breasts and the actress tells him that is quite all right. She is not troubled at all. They shoot the "domestic" version, but then they move on to a "European" version in which the action becomes more extensive and another actress is called in in the afternoon—a body double—not as pleasant, but perfectly competent.

"Where is this in the story?" the young actor asks the director.

"Don't worry. Fucking fits anywhere," he is reassured.

The workmanlike frenzy mounts. He is shooting every day now, and often there are several scenes on the same day. Nothing seems to fit. He is given scraps of paper with lines of dialogue, and sometimes they are typed. But there is still no script, and no way for him to know where different moments occur in "the arc"—he has heard this term used often. He cannot fathom the order of events or the development of his character, so the frenzy is like a coma in which all the things are simultaneous. One day he has a scene with the girlfriend again, though she has a child now, and he asks her how this scene fits with the one already done where they make love.

"I think that's been cut," she says. "I'm sorry. I liked it." And she smiles in an encouraging way that might be her character's fondness.

Two days later, she tells him, "I was wrong. The sex is back, and we may get a lot more." She sounds shy about it.

But there is no more. Instead, other characters and storylines jostle for time and a place, and the young actor does his best to be blown along by the wind called schedule. He realizes that he has appearance and presence in the film, but nothing that could be called character. He believes it is chaos, and when the film opens (with the last part of his dollar turning up promptly) he sees scenes in it where he is apparently talking to people he never met.

The movie is reviewed, and there are remarks about its "surreal inner cohesion." He is asked whether he would like to make another film, about a character who has been hit on the head and lost all memory. Why not? he replies.[1]

ACT **IV**

That Night

Midsummer night. In the Count's Kitchen.

ithout work, actors seethe with stories, as if they were ordinary, hopeful folks. Along came the first part this actor had ever had for which his name appeared in the credits. The first that he could see as a turning point in the picture.

"It is not such a big thing," said his director. "A moment really. But I will tell you that in my experience the cinema is a matter of moments—a glimpse, a glance, an unexpected gesture."

"Yes, I see," said the young actor.

"Read it," advised the director. "A young man sees a woman in the street, and then this is the text:

"Owing to the impatient strain in my nature, which has often led me astray, I found myself walking towards her with a smile of welcome, but in those few instants I was already overwhelmed by the perfectly clear consciousness that I might neither talk to her nor greet her in any manner."[1]

"Do you see?" asked the director. "It's yes and no, a tracking shot across your path, with your whole being turning to see her. About to utter but hushed. The camera moves one way—you turn to look the other way. It's provocative. Motion bearing emotion."

"The camera is itself an actor?" the young actor realized.

"That's all there is to it," said the director. He was breathless with vision.

The young actor considered the situation. He thought himself into that slanting camera and a wheeling point of attention. But he studied too hard. It was as if he halted motion.

"That's too obvious," said the director, after the first two takes. "It was spelled out. You knew you were going to be surprised."

"Ah, yes," said the actor. "If I had someone to notice, perhaps?"

"Of course."

A young woman was picked out of the crowd, a passerby, with wild brown hair. She blushed on being asked; she tried to tidy that irrepressible hair—have you ever known hair that is most becoming when unrestrained? She had only to walk—she would not be on film. The actor shook her hand. He would marry her before the year was out.

"Oh, yes!" said the director after the third take. "That was splendid! I believe I may enlarge your part. Are you free the rest of the week?"

And the woman smiled at the young actor as if she expected no less.

In the matter of faith, some people have shattering epiphanies: they are struck down in a fit on the road to somewhere or other; they write an oratorio or begin to build an immense fanciful cathedral that can never be finished. Others do not mention their own soul to another person. It may be that the cult of acting has encouraged many professionals to be sensations, show-offs, or mad. While others conceal their disturbance and go about life hushed and grave. It's a way of looking at ourselves and at actors.

I do not mean to condemn or despair of actors who tear down

the theatre in their passion. But there are some who go about the job as if it was a matter of carpentry or bookkeeping. Take Michael Bryant.

Bryant was born in 1928 and he died in 2002. For twenty-five years, he was a regular at the National Theatre, though often in supporting parts. He was Polonius in that Daniel Day-Lewis *Hamlet* that I have talked about. He was not beautiful, I daresay, but he was versatile and utterly reliable (those two things do not always go together). He had great moments as a young man: he was the central character, Mathieu, in a thirteen-part TV adaptation of Jean-Paul Sartre's *The Roads to Freedom* (1972), and he had played with Judi Dench in a famous television production, *Talking to a Stranger* (1966), written by John Hopkins. Early on he had been Willie the man from Harvard in the original London production of *The Iceman Cometh*. Much later he played Prospero for Peter Hall. There was also a scarcely known but intense TV play, *Mille Miglia* (1968), in which he was the race-car driver Stirling Moss—written by Athol Fugard. He was Teddy, the professor come home, in the original London production of Pinter's *The Homecoming*.

There is not a Michael Bryant memoir or biography. If you look up the name on Amazon, you find a Canadian Michael Bryant who wrote a best-seller about addiction and justice. I doubt that Michael Bryant ever delivered his credo on acting in a major interview. Walking on the promenade at the South Bank in London you might have passed him by without noticing. He made some movies, but in the nature of things his most heartfelt work may not survive. So let's say he was still somewhere between reliable and sublime (again, those two are not common fits). I don't know that he ever threw a fit of dramatic temperament, interrupted a rehearsal with cries of outrage, or was late. All I can find is that during *Talking to a Stranger* and its emotional strain he was known to ease Judi Dench and jolly her along. And one other thing: in that crucial *Hamlet* where Day-Lewis walked away, Dench (who was Gertrude) found Bryant in a corridor backstage crying his eyes out. Dench took him to his dressing room and held him like a baby as he sobbed. To be so moved.[2]

The director on that show, Richard Eyre, thought Bryant "as reluctant to theorise about acting as about a piece of wood or a cow." Bryant, in every apparent way, treated his craft as a trade, something learned and not to be fussed over. He observed life and drew from it, in a methodical way. "He talks little in rehearsal and needs, or wants, only the most basic information—where he is to stand, what the furniture is, louder, softer, quicker, slower. He regards the text as the only hard evidence at his disposal, and matter-of-factly builds his character like a detective assembling a case until one day, sometimes alarmingly late in rehearsal, the character is there—complete."[3]

But he sobbed once when a fellow actor broke down.

I suggested earlier the anomaly of so few characters in Shakespeare attached to God or religious faith in a period of English history when such things meant life and death. Not that this seems to have been held against him by that fraction of Elizabethan and Jacobean people who saw his plays. Though in the age of Puritan intensity that came not long after Shakespeare there were fierce campaigns fought against acting and the evils of theatre. But the originality of theatre as Shakespeare constructed it is the dramatization of a questioning mind, or of people who have made disastrous decisions and must live with the consequences. The Ghost of his father has no religious resonance. Hamlet recognizes few moral answers in wondering what to do (though he cooks up the story of Claudius being at prayer for a reason not to kill him). The Ghost is a theatrical device, of course, but he is the projection of Hamlet's unease, his imaginative intelligence, his paranoia, his dread, his need for redemptive action, and his attempt to believe in family. And so, over the centuries, there have been so many ways of playing the Ghost that reflect Hamlet's indecision or madness. That the play works, and worked from the beginning, was because it found an audience fascinated by the ontological indecision of this smart, lonely humanist figure. He may be the first existentialist in our literature, and so it is no wonder that the role has become a test for actors just as the play is still a terminus in the history of dramatic literature. We cannot take our eyes off his magnetic solitude, and the soliloquy is the literary form that expresses his talking to himself. It worked on stage, with the actor coming to the brink of his audience, in some isolating light. That technology was unwitting rehearsal for the thing we call cinema, so when Olivier did his *Hamlet* in 1948, the camera gazed at his soulful face while the actor only spoke the lines on the invisible soundtrack.

Olivier's *Hamlet* has dated—anything as sensational and current as acting is likely to lose its ripeness. And that prompts an uneasy consideration: that 1948 *Hamlet* is preserved (more or less)—we can see the film and feel Olivier's self-rapture, the special romantic pessimism of the postwar years, and the almost inescapable self-pity that accompanies dramatic earnestness on film. But in 1948 that film was astonishing: it took on a Shakespeare play with unexpected fidelity and made it like a film noir; and it carried the crowd. Still, it's not as provocative or touching as the best Hamlets you may have seen in the years since. So that *Hamlet* is exposed by the way it survives, as inert as old film. The movie of *Streetcar* is strong and intact, but am I alone in feeling the magic resides in the first Broadway version? I have a friend who admires the Lear Paul Scofield filmed for Peter Brook. Ah, he sighs, but Scofield's Lear on stage—something that is now fifty-two years ago and unrecorded—that was finer. Yet my friend cannot remember why. He is left to know it.

Consider another comparison: in 1980, at the Old Vic in London, Peter O'Toole did a *Macbeth*.[4] The production proved one of the famous calamities, and justification for the theatrical regard for the dire bad luck attached to that play. It was meant to offer fresh life for the Old Vic as a theatre. But O'Toole was ill, badly affected by drink, and without the physical or nervous energy he had once possessed. That did not stop him having a fierce but obscure sense of what the play was about. He seemed obsessed with its witchcraft. One director quit. His replacement, the filmmaker Bryan Forbes, was not strong enough to challenge O'Toole's will. There was confusion over the sets and a reckless decision to have the play awash in blood. Long before it premiered, there were terrible doubts, but no one could negotiate with O'Toole or even understand what he wanted. The show opened—O'Toole insisted on calling it "Harry Lauder" instead of *Macbeth,* because of the superstition attached to the Scottish play. The production was a great disaster, and on the first night the audience dismay turned to helpless laughter. The actors battled on (Frances Tomelty as Lady Macbeth seems to have been in courageous denial of what was going on around her).

The reviews were dreadful and mocking. And the audience fought for tickets. The show sold out—because people were intrigued to see a ruin, bored with accomplished *Macbeth*s, or even because as the run went on something emerged in O'Toole that began to redeem the early chaos? We don't know, but "chaos is come again" is a Shakespearean principle. That O'Toole *Macbeth* was never recorded, never put on film—and probably most people reckoned that was a sound decision, a mercy to all those concerned. But still, calamity is alluring (and theatrical), and true legend may depend on the lack of substance or reference. Is it possible that all acting on film dates, while any lost performance begins to thrive?

I noted earlier that Stephen Sondheim has been conscious of keeping a record of a production. He has said that he had never seen his musical *Passion* (first done in 1994) come into proper focus until the Donmar Warehouse revival in London in 2010. For the first time, he felt, the story was about Giorgio, and not Fosca—this may be another version of whether *Streetcar* is about Stanley or Blanche. Sondheim wrote about his regret that the Donmar version was never filmed:

> I remembered a conversation I'd had in 1979 at a large cocktail party given for Tony award nominees, where I found myself haranguing

two of the most accomplished directors in the British theatre, deploring the fact that plays and musicals in London were not being preserved for posterity the way they were in New York, where Lincoln Center Library for the Performing Arts had been videotaping productions both on and off Broadway since 1970. The Britishers were surprised, not to say baffled. Preservation had never crossed their minds, they said—why would anyone want to freeze an art that by definition keeps changing shape? The whole point of theatre is that every performance is unique; the play may be the same from night to night but not the performance.[5]

It sounds like life again—which cannot be a bad thing—and it seems to capture an essential dilemma we have with acting, not just as audiences beholding it and coming to some opinion, but as people in the large, untidy play of life who must try to work out what is happening. Most of my professional work has involved commenting on film performances—the many notable pieces of work by actors and actresses, from Gary Cooper to Regis Toomey, but also the generality of what happens to a performance that is frozen or stopped against time.

The history is telling. When Hamlet meets the Players and instructs them in doing Gonzago's Revenge (with an extra speech he will supply), his advice to them is not far from what any ideal director would say today. It could embrace Olivier and Lee Strasberg: it wants both naturalism *and* a piercing coup. More or less, the directors of actors have said the same things forever, depending on their kindness and the variation they have found in actors. You can see how movie directors might relish escaping into the impassive eloquence of the camera. But the players who have come to Elsinore are unnamed. Do they roam the world?

If so, how are they supported? They are part of that world of performance in which the players are no better known than the members of an orchestra. We assumed they had skill and dedication, and we gave them dinner when we could.

In the age of Garrick and Kean actors became better known, even if the public had little knowledge of what they were like. They might be nearly as popular as Charles Dickens, who was famous as a performer of his own work, so fond of theatre that he insisted on appearing on stage. In and just after his time, the status of actors and their reach changed—because of the photograph. People could buy postcards of Sarah Bernhardt, and so she posed for some of the leading photographers of her day. She even made a few films, though these cannot give an adequate sense of what she must have been like. Still, she was one of the most famous people in the world in the late nineteenth century—for her quality, but also because of her zeal in self-promotion and her belief in her own "divineness."

It is a famous, comic confession of the infant picture business that it found itself besieged, in 1900, and thereafter, by eager audiences asking, "Who was that? No, not her, the third bathing beauty from the left?" Early pictures, or photoplays, did not bother to identify the performers or grasp how quickly audiences were falling for them. It's easy enough to say that that girl in an Edwardian swimming costume seemed prettier, perter, or even sexier than the others. But, more than that, people were beginning to be drawn to something we can only call an arresting inwardness. Maybe men in the audience dreamed of flirting with some of the Mack Sennett girls, or going farther—though

I don't think the dream was that bold or lubricious yet. But another desire was at work: it was simply to be *with* some image—Mabel Normand, Chaplin, Doug Fairbanks, Mary Pickford—or to share in the inner life that was there on the surface of those pool-like eyes. We wanted to be the movie people. We identified with them. Had people felt that way about *Hamlet* in 1602, or Mozart's *Figaro* in 1786? We don't know. But consider that that vicarious enterprise, the wish to be on or in the screen, did not occur until the invention of photography and the close-up prompted it. It offered a kind of intimacy that had never existed before. With silent film, that interaction was accelerated; but with sound, our detachment was gone, and our loneliness seemed softened. The screen was a ghost world that was our private party.

The picture business seized on this habit—and recollect that for a few years after 1895 it was not clear that the new craze would lead to a business. But soon enough commerce labeled these rare faces (it often gave them names that were not their own), paid them and put them under contract. So the history of the movies involves a special kind of employment, promotion, and servitude in which the people who were made stars belonged to production studios, were trained and perfected by them, were publicized, protected, and lied about, and were put in steady work in stories, or vehicles, that were deemed suitable for them, but which often crushed the spirit of the players and seemed like a kind of slavery. Of course, the public laughed at that: what kind of slavery was it that brought fame, $300,000 a year, and a life in Beverly Hills? Moreover, how did those kids have the nerve to complain when they lacked the talent or resources to step out on a stage and be heard, let alone attended to? But they were so owned and sheltered that the part of life made of independence was denied them. Some observers noted that they were like pampered children.

This range of talent varied: Chaplin had excelled on the music-hall stage. Bette Davis, Spencer Tracy, and many others had had impressive stage careers before sound took them to Hollywood. Some actors in that tradition never gave up on the theatre —Fredric March did plays long after his movie stardom began (he was the first Tyrone in *Long Day's Journey into Night*); and in Britain the generation of Olivier, Gielgud, and Richardson tended to regard the movies as a lucky bonus for their real calling. Still, there are icons of the screen who never ventured on a stage or questioned the assumption that they could not have survived there—Joan Crawford (she did dance in a few musicals), Jean Harlow, John Wayne, Clint Eastwood. I do not mean to say those people would have been lost or an embarrassment on stage—in the way of Madonna, say, in the 1988 Broadway premiere of David Mamet's *Speed the Plow*. When John Wayne came down a long staircase at the Academy Awards and announced that *The Deer Hunter* had won best picture, he seemed confident in his command of that space, but it was his last public appearance. Maybe Clint could have played James Tyrone. Maybe he thought it saner to avoid the opportunity or the risk and simply held to the economic system he had acquired in making pictures. A sadder truth is that, after *Streetcar,* Marlon Brando never returned to the challenge of the stage (apart from a modest and brief Boston production of Shaw's *Man and Superman* in 1954). Time and again, the Method was preparation for the movies.

Brando took that decision himself, for he arrived in Hollywood just as the studio contract system was breaking apart. But for thirty years before then, actors had been properties. Signed on long-term contracts, they had done the movies to which they were assigned. Their faces might be remade along with their names; they were taught to diet, dress, speak, dance, and ride horseback; they "gave" interviews for the fan magazines—or they signed off on interviews written by the publicity department. Altogether, they colluded in a fraudulent bill of sale for an impossible intimacy. They posed for candid pictures. They were helped in burying unduly truthful or scandalous events—awkward affairs, driving problems (Clark Gable killed a pedestrian), ugly family stories, or unfortunate habits. As in their films, so the publicity kept them adorable. It was a total presentation, always backed up by signed glossy photographs—for the still photograph was the simple version of the screen, a slippery token of identity, to be held in your hand as you fantasized over some him or her. Long before politics had recognized its own need for the elaborate cover-up or makeover, show business and the movies had been working out its schematics.

Something else happened to acting in the postwar years. Just as people in New York found Stanley Kowalski startlingly "real," so this other event was easily called "realism." The experience of war, genocide, and poverty had left many people ashamed of the shining light and eager happiness of entertainment films. It was time for reality. Nowhere was that urge stronger than in Italy, where the theory was strengthened by a lack of resources for filmmaking. Who could afford to pay actors? So in 1947–48, the director Vittorio De Sica and his writer, Cesare Zavattini, made a picture called *Ladri di Biciclette—Bicycle Thieves.* In Rome, a poor family is desperate for the man, the husband and the father, to have a job. He has a chance to be employed sticking up posters for big movies. But he can't do the job without a bicycle. So the family sell their precious bed linen to get a cycle. But then, as he is putting up a poster for Rita Hayworth in *Gilda,* the bicycle is stolen.

De Sica had difficulty raising money for this plain story. So he paid for the picture himself. Resolved not to have anyone with the polished manner of a professional, he cast an ordinary factory worker, Lamberto Maggiorani, who had never acted before.

This common man had a "good face"—whatever that means. He could be photographed, and I daresay De Sica would have replaced any factory worker who turned out to be stricken with self-consciousness, or simple lack of expressiveness. So this amateur was a natural, if you like. But De Sica (who had been an actor himself for years) had faith in the ability of many ordinary people to do a decent job in a movie. So it proved. *Bicycle Thieves* was a spectacular box office event all over the world. It was a special success in America, to such a point that David O. Selznick thought of doing an American remake, with Cary Grant as the man. That idea was lost, but Maggiorani did have a career as an actor for a dozen years before he and the world acknowledged that really he didn't have the necessary talent or an Olivier-like freedom in pretending.

Bicycle Thieves had cost a little more than $100,000. It made a small fortune, and by 1952 the magazine *Sight and Sound* had voted it the greatest film ever made. Its influence was enormous, and it confirmed an old notion—one that went back as far as Greek theatre and masked players—that in the proper dramatic situation, a simple human presence was enough. Even in the strenuous pursuit of naturalistic gesture in acting that we associate with the Method, there was a theory afoot that said, no, nothing, do nothing at all—any attempt to be credible is intrusive and vulgar. Long before this, the Russian theorist and director Lev Kuleshov had made an experiment in which a single close-up of an actor—without script, direction, or instruction—could be cross-cut with shots of, say, a bowl of hot soup, a child, or a threatening dog, and the result was a feeling of hunger, tenderness, or fear. Those feelings didn't have to be acted, because the audience knew the syntax in advance. They had felt it in life.[6]

A few years after *Bicycle Thieves,* these principles found their best demonstration in the films of Robert Bresson. He was a great artist, an essential figure in film history with *Diary of a Country Priest, A Man Escaped* and *Pickpocket.* What is germane here is that Bresson did not like or feel comfortable with professional actors. He cast amateurs, or people never seen before. It is true that they had "good" faces, but it is also true that he gave them very little guidance. They understood the situation—in *A Man Escaped,* Robert Leterrier plays Fontane, a resistance fighter imprisoned by the Gestapo and wondering whether he will be executed before he can manage to escape.

Bresson would write: "It is not a matter of acting 'simple' or of acting 'inward' but of not acting at all." He preferred to call his players "models," and he asked for them to be "mechanized outwardly. Intact, virgin within."[7] It is not a theory that amuses professional actors, and Bresson knew that he would never use anyone more than once—because the public would supply the career history to any later appearance (and this is the essence of stardom), and because the models would have looked at themselves and turned into cute copyists.

The cinema of Robert Bresson is enough to make the theory intriguing. Even if it seems to undermine the career of acting, it is an idea that seems more profound and useful than all the defenses of the Method put together. Once you have it in your mind, it begins to be possible to look at performances and see the Bressonian truth at work. I have no idea whether Philip Seymour Hoffman had read Bresson or seen his films, but I think in some of his best work he is on the verge of trusting himself to do "nothing." And you may need to know or feel a lot to do nothing.

Then again, if you're talking to your beloved, she is not going to be content with so little.

Why Does Acting Matter?

You are having an important job interview. You are meeting a person of one sex or other, without knowing yet how significant the relationship may prove to be. You are in the offices of a movie studio pitching a story to them; it might rescue the studio and do you no harm. Or, in an idle part of a summer afternoon, in a remote part of the forest, you are simply trying to observe yourself as a way of understanding this curious role you have been assigned. Will nothing suffice?[8]

You consider what you should wear to the interview. You may purchase a new tie with the right mixture of splendor and dignity. You shine your shoes; you have a fresh haircut; you consider what you might say if a prospective employer happens to ask, "Tell us about yourself." The would-be lover could ask the same question. You are intent on presenting yourself in everyday life. You give the matter consideration—in a way, it has been the central task of your life since consciousness set in. You know you want to make an impression; you want to be clear, eloquent, and persuasive; you want to be understood and liked. You want company, the very word that describes the loose family of actors.

You are not inclined to lie in the interview or with a potential lover. You have some notion of being true to yourself, and even if you do not believe that God is watching you—as some of our ancestors took for granted—still you have absorbed that process of scrutiny for yourself. You probably decide not to lie—for lying is a tougher test on memory than telling the truth. But that does not bar you from "creating" your character. You know that you need to present yourself well, as if an actor were playing you. It is the job of your life. It is why you consider what to say and how to say it. You have noticed that certain things to say—true enough—do not work, or convince others. So you rewrite your script. It is your equation of backstory with your open future. And if you are doing this in 2015, then you are the fourth or fifth generation that has had a lifelong training of watching actors—at the movies, on television, on stage.

There was a time—not so long ago—when most people never saw actors. But throughout the twentieth century that innocence was swept aside. For sixty years now, nearly all of us have spent several hours a day watching actors, or screened people. For some of us, on some days, we spend more time with acted figures than with real people.

You probably never meant to be an actor yourself, in the professional sense, yet you are steeped in the awareness that a smile, a silence, a pause, or a sigh are all things that will be read as signs of character and intent. That is how you look at other people; that is how you assume they study you. Put this bluntly it may sound like the threshold of falsehood and deception. This can happen. But most of us work hard to be sincere (without seeming earnest, or solemn, or saved). If we can do it naturally. One way or another, we have absorbed and we embody Hamlet's advice to the players, "to hold, as 'twere, the mirror up to nature."

But if Hamlet knew this, and if he deliberately set out to be different Hamlets for different people at Elsinore, have humans always had this instinct?

Probably, but we do not know. It is my estimate that the instinct and the skills have simply become more far-reaching and subtle since the onset of those visual forms of communication that told us we were being looked at and studied. We have had to do this because in the increasing crowd self-awareness may be our defense against fears of anonymity. But that pressure towards loss of identity increases all the time, and so the process of acting becomes more necessary as an assurance that we exist. There is a further problem: as an actor takes on more and more characters, the inner self may be like a room to rent—a space where every successive tenant brings his own furniture and color scheme, his own definition of being "at home." Is that why actors so often keep the company of other actors? Is there something in the condition, like a malady, that means outsiders can never grasp the insecurity?

Why acting matters? Could it be that we fall apart without it? But does that mean that all our experiences have become like scenes from the play of our lives? After all, very soon we will be gone, and are we then a play that was never recorded? For a while, perhaps, survivors in our audience will say, "Oh, he was like that. She was that sort of person." But very soon that small crowd will be blown away like dust. Go back two hundred years in most families, and you have no more idea of who people were or what they were like than you have of those who will come two hundred years from now. But all of us, at the time, for a moment, are the center of attention. We all were Hamlet. History and destiny turned on our leverage. Until we vanished, so soon enough it hardly matters whether Burbage's Macbeth was better than Peter O'Toole's, or ours. Our companionship has a few shared things—breathing air, feeling sexuality, hunger, and loneliness. But many of us know the desolation that only acting can keep at bay.

So, wait, here comes a stranger. I must greet him, and be my best version of myself.

Listen to Claire Bloom. In her time she played Juliet and Blanche DuBois. She acted with Chaplin, Olivier, Burton and . . . well, perhaps with her husbands. In that ongoing work, she had a challenging cast: Rod Steiger, the brother in the back of the cab in *On the Waterfront;* Hillard Elkins, a producer; and Philip Roth, who one day wrote a novel about an actress he was married to, named Claire. He was not kind to her in the book and did not seem to be impressed by her. She was terribly hurt, of course, yet in an odd way his estimate matched her own:

When you work in the theatre, you have no day at all—your performance hangs over you all day long. If it's a comedy or a light role, it's not so bad, but if it's a taxing or difficult role and you're doing it eight times a week, you've got to be careful. If you manage to crawl out on your hands and knees and have lunch and have a little walk, that's fine. If you meet someone, or if you want to go to a shop or a museum, well, that's difficult, because you must be resting by four and up again at five to get to the theatre by six-thirty, assuming the performance is at eight. And when it's over, you can't go straight to bed. It's the only time of the day you're hungry, and you want to eat and to drink and talk to your friends and have a good time; if you don't have that then, you don't have it at all. So you don't get to bed until one or two, and ideally, you shouldn't wake up until eleven. In London, when the day is short and it's dark at four and you don't get out of the house till twelve-thirty or one, it's like living in the city of dreadful night. On a matinee day you get up, you have a very light lunch, you go to the theatre, you do the performance, you have an avocado, you go to sleep and then you wake up—you try to wake up—to do the next performance. If you're playing in repertory and have a couple of nights off, then you have a way of stoking yourself up again. But in the commercial theatre, if you have two performances on Saturday, they leave you totally exhausted on Sunday. And by Monday morning, when you're beginning to feel better, it starts again.[9]

To which one might only add two things:

What if you have a spouse and children, expecting their scenes?

Plus, Claire Bloom did not do too much comedy. If she had she might have known the saying, "Dying is easy. Comedy is hard," which is attributed to nearly everyone from Edmund Kean to Peter O'Toole. But, of course, O'Toole took the extra risk of playing *Macbeth* for laughs.

The proximity of drama and farce can be too close to be bearable. By 1895, Henry James was established. His list of published works included *Washington Square* (which would live to be adapted as a very successful play, *The Heiress*), *The Aspern Papers,* and *The Portrait of a Lady,* about which it would be hard to write a paragraph without using the word "dramatic." In *The Heiress* (made into a play by Ruth and Augustus Goetz), the contest between Dr. Austin Sloper and his plain and rich daughter Catherine is always gripping. It opened on Broadway in 1947, with Basil Rathbone and Wendy Hiller; in London, it was Ralph Richardson and Peggy Ashcroft. There was a film, in 1950, directed by William Wyler, with Richardson and Olivia de Havilland. There have been so many revivals, including a film by Agnieszka Holland with Albert Finney and Jennifer Jason Leigh. The material is robust enough to survive even its most recent and inept iteration, with David Strathairn and Jessica Chastain. It is surefire, a natural, and it is clearly Henry James.

Why not, for he was deeply drawn to theatre. Living in England, he was ambitious to write for the stage from the mid-1880s, and remained so for close to twenty years. Was that because of the fame and wealth that might attend theatrical success? Or was it that a man essentially committed to the privacy of writing fiction was helplessly attracted to the prospect of being with actors who could realize his dreams? Writers cherish actors. They have said the words themselves first, under their breath. They have faced the alternative directions for the action. It can be uncanny to find flesh and blood that approximates your words. Writers sometimes make ghastly misjudgments when they meet actors—think of Arthur Miller, John Osborne, Harold Pinter, the list goes on.

The reality can be alarming. In rehearsal for *Guy Domville,* James wrote to a friend, "I may have been meant for the Drama—God knows!—but I certainly wasn't meant for the Theatre."[10] *Domville* is a play about a man preparing for the priesthood who decides to marry. I doubt I will ever see it produced, and if I did I might just be part of the reception James suffered in January 1895:

> The delicate, picturesque, extremely human & extremely artistic little play, was taken profanely by a brutal & ill-disposed gallery which had shown signs of malice prepense from the 1st & which, held in hand till the end, kicked up an infernal row at the fall of the curtain. There followed an abominable ¼ of an hour during wh. all the forces of civilization in the house waged a battle of the most gallant, prolonged & sustained applause with the hoots & jeers & catcalls of the roughs, whose roars (like those of a cage of beasts at some infernal "Zoo") were only exacerbated (as it were!) by the conflict. It was a char[m]ing scene, as you may imagine, for a nervous, sensitive, exhausted author to face.[11]

Guy Domville ran only a few weeks and was followed on stage at the St. James's Theatre by the premiere of *The Importance of Being Earnest.*

James was quickly disenchanted. Within a month, he was telling the editor of *Century* magazine that no, he could not write an appreciation of Eleanora Duse, whom he had seen several times. He was against contributing to "the ridiculous abandonment of all proportion & perspective in the worship of the *actor & actress,* the deification of their little 3d-rate personalities, the colossal inflation of them by the gigantic bellows of the Press."[12] And yet, only a few years earlier James had written a novel, *The Tragic Muse,* that includes among its characters Miriam Rooth, a young actress who is determined to improve her art and make a career. The novel is not a complete success, but Miriam is so alive you know how much her creator had thought about acting.

In a book not meant to be long, I knew I could never find room for all the actors who deserved to be here—not if I was going to cover Regis Toomey properly. So I decided to follow a few test cases through the book; and because they seemed by general consent to be the two most striking and ambitious players of recent times, I chose Laurence Olivier and Marlon Brando (with Vivien Leigh as their link). They can seem like opposites, yet I hope I have suggested with some plausibility that they were not just alike, or even rivals, but actors who might sometimes have exchanged parts in the way actors have taken turns at being Othello and Iago. If Olivier would have been stealthy and impressive in *The Godfather,* wouldn't Brando have made an impassioned and dangerous Othello—if he and some management had been prepared to let him put on blackface? No one really rebuked Olivier for that in 1964 (though the production never went to America). Ten years later, Brando might have been attacked for doing the same thing.

Brando was seventeen years younger than Olivier. He was from a prairie city, Omaha, Nebraska, while Olivier was born in Dorking, in Surrey, a country town to the south of London. The places seem very different, but the boys had things in common: mothers who doted on them, and distant fathers who disapproved. They had issues with honesty and how to deal with it. Marlon realized that his mother was drinking, and it troubled him. As he describes it, you can begin to see how pain and confusion formed him:

> When my mother drank, her breath had a sweetness that I lack the vocabulary to describe. It was a strange marriage, the sweetness of her breath and my hatred of her drinking. She was always sipping surreptitiously from her bottle of Empirin, which she called "my change-of-life medicine." It was usually filled with gin. As I got older, occasionally I would find myself with a woman whose breath had that sweetness that still defies description. I was always sexually aroused by the smell. As much as I hated it, it had an undeniable allure for me.[13]

Larry's distress in growing up came differently. At an early age, by five or six, he lied. Sometimes it was for a reason, but often—he said—it was nature or habit, done for its own sake. So his very fond mother beat him for being dishonest. Beat him? I suspect he exaggerated. Perhaps she spanked him lightly. He saw that having to do this distressed her. So he stopped lying—for a while. But then it resumed and matured. In his autobiography, *Confessions of an Actor,* he tells this on himself:

> Nowadays [1982] people often ask my wife, Joan, "How do you know when Larry's acting, and when he's not?" and my wife will always reply, "Larry? Oh, he's acting all the time." In my heart of hearts I only know that I am far from sure when I am acting and when I am not or, should I more frankly put it, when I am lying and when I am not? For what is acting but lying, and what is good acting but convincing lying?[14]

One can imagine the look of horror on Brando's face at that. He clung to a prospect of truth, and when he did *Last Tango in Paris,* he willingly contributed his own experiences growing up to his character, Paul, and anguished over it in extended improvisations. In a way that is an apogee of Method acting. The gap between the two men reflected changing attitudes. The standard for truth or realism in acting shifted so that many people saw Brando as more modern than Olivier, more in tune with rough, unschooled emotional existence. So Olivier could not have attempted *Last Tango in Paris,* which is usually regarded as one of Brando's most daring and personal works. Equally, I don't think Brando could have managed the theatrical wickedness of *Richard III* or the utterly American class consciousness of Hurstwood in *Carrie.* Yet both actors loved risk and danger, and a feeling for challenge that might have encouraged any attempt. Brando's Fletcher Christian in *Mutiny on the Bounty* could be cousin to Olivier's Nelson in *That Hamilton Woman,* even if Olivier might have winced at Brando's English accent. Near the end of his life, Brando taught strange acting classes under the rubric, "Lying for a Living." What would you have given to see them together as Vladimir and Estragon, the tramps in *Waiting for Godot*?

No one would deny or impeach Brando's genius. In offering the possibility that Olivier could have done an intriguing Vito Corleone, I don't think he would have been as effortlessly moving as Brando managed. And "effortlessly" is the key word—for, in the Wellesian sense, I doubt Brando needed to feel power or triumph as much as Olivier. But could Brando have captured the resplendent self-loathing in Olivier's Archie Rice, without being ruined? All of which is odd, for whereas Olivier seems never to have tired of self-admiration, Brando succumbed to its opposite.

Almost as soon as he triumphed on screen, after his Oscar for *On the Waterfront,* Brando's movies declined. He never worked with Kazan again: the actor said he was horrified at his director's testimony naming old associates as Communists; he may also have been needled by the fuss over James Dean, and Kazan taking on a new protégé. He became disenchanted with Hollywood, and he never managed to take charge of his own career. He did not find his own material, or mount his own productions, and by the late 1950s such things were common in American film. The most notable failure, and perhaps the most crushing, was the director walking away from *One-Eyed Jacks.* Was that a lack of stamina or persistence, or a failure as an organizing storyteller?

By contrast, Olivier directed and organized his three Shakespeare films—*Henry V, Hamlet,* and *Richard III*—and would never have dreamed of quitting. *The Prince and the Showgirl,* with Marilyn Monroe, was an ordeal, and ended up a dismal picture, but Olivier was resolutely professional. Of course, he had another flag, that of the National Theatre. Olivier hardly ever joined political or social causes. But the National was an old dream in Britain that had been dismissed by many of its best enthusiasts. Olivier's record there as director was not flawless. But he endured the years of committees and bureaucracy, the compromises and the interruptions to his other life as an actor, and the National is there still on the South Bank, a working monument and museum, with the largest auditorium named after him (1,150 seats). It's hard to believe that anyone else had the authority, the tenacity, and the need for victory to bring that off. He made enemies; he always had. But countless strangers know that the National on the South Bank reshaped London and has been a focus for British theatre greater than Stratford-on-Avon.

It's not difficult now to dislike Olivier the man, but his achievement is Nelsonian. There was something to be said for his resolve to be victorious, and a brazen liar, even if it sometimes restricted him as an actor to calculated effects and a superior coldness. In 1945–46, he had established his postwar eminence with a characteristic tour de force. In the same evening, he played *Oedipus* and then Mr. Puff in Sheridan's *The Critic,* a satire on acting. The first role was far larger than the second. Oedipus was blinded and ruined and Olivier gave him a momentous groan that made audiences shudder. He said he thought of it by imagining the horror of an ermine caught in a trap. After the interval he became a white-faced Mr. Puff in a dainty comedy of manners. The transformation could hardly be greater (and it was Olivier who had insisted on *The Critic,* against the wishes of director Tyrone Guthrie). Here was such versatility as to mock the notion that an actor needs to sink into one part and then lives with it for a long time afterwards. This, more or less, was how Vivien Leigh would react to the ordeal of *Streetcar*. But listen to Olivier exulting in his range and defying the theory of prolonged immersion. (This is the man who, years later, despairing of Dustin Hoffman's cogitative delays on *Marathon Man,* dispelled the American's Actors Studio training by an aside to the director, John Schlesinger, "Oh, gracious, why doesn't the dear boy just act?")

> The gift of playing in *The Critic,* following immediately upon *Oedipus,* worked like a dream for me. I could really sink myself deep into the Greek tragedy without reservation, secure in the anticipation of the joyous gaiety that was to follow it. I felt I was in for the greatest enjoyment ever allowed me in the work of acting (I was still under the thrall of having directed the film of *Henry V*).[15]

He took pleasure in repeating the joke about the spectacular evening being called "Oedipuff."

It's impossible to find such satisfaction in Brando. As his career went on, he was beset by mishaps, many of his own making, some as he would have said the consequence of a righteous man trying to survive in Hollywood. He had a very public divorce from Anna Kashfi and a bitter dispute over custody of their child, Christian. Brando identified with so many good causes, but then he made an idiot of himself by sending Sacheen Littlefeather to collect and refuse his second Oscar, for *The Godfather.* Moreover, he had obtained that part because of the determined support of Francis Coppola. But when he saw a cut of the film, he so misjudged it that he traded in his profit points for a pittance in immediate cash. That made him the more bitter afterwards. He took on *Last Tango* and played long scenes with a naked Maria Schneider. But then he declined director Bernardo Bertolucci's request that he be naked, too. Later on in life, his son Christian killed the young man who was lover and abuser to his half-sister Cheyenne. Christian was tried and jailed and Marlon was in tears on the witness stand. Cheyenne committed suicide a few years later. By then, Marlon had put on so much weight that he was often referred to as a hulk. The only other American actor who had exchanged such beauty for huge overweight was Orson Welles, and in both men there was a savage accompanying disappointment with life and their work.[16]

Brando became cynical, and perhaps his saddest fall was when he turned up unprepared and out of shape to play Colonel Kurtz in *Apocalypse Now* for the director, Francis Coppola, who had done so much to rescue him with *The Godfather*. This is how Brando described that work in his book *Songs My Mother Taught Me:*

> I told Francis I thought that the first time the audience hears Kurtz, his voice should come out of the darkness. After several long moments, he should make an entrance in which only his bald head is visible; then a small part of his face is lit before he returns to the shadows. In a sense the same process is going on in Kurtz's mind: he is in darkness and shadows, drifting back and forth in the netherworld he has created for himself in the jungle; he no longer has any moral frame of reference in this surreal world, which is a perfect parable of the insane Vietnam War.
>
> I was good at bullshitting Francis and persuading him to think my way, and he bought it, but what I'd really wanted from the beginning was to find a way to make my part smaller so that I wouldn't have to work as hard. . . .
>
> Besides restructuring the plot, I wrote Kurtz's speeches, includ-

ing a monologue at his death that must have been forty-five minutes long. It was probably the closest I've ever come to getting lost in a part, and one of the best scenes I've ever played because I really had to hold myself under control. I made it up extemporaneously, bringing up images like a snail crawling along the edge of a razor. I was hysterical: I cried and laughed, and it was a wonderful scene. Francis shot it twice—two 45-minute improvisations—but used hardly any of the footage in the picture. I thought it was effective, though it might have been out of place. I never saw the footage of the entire speech, so I wouldn't know.[17]

That resignation, the ultimate defeat of interest, is very Brando. Perhaps they were great scenes or monstrous delaying tactics, some sort of jazzy "To be or not to be," a signal to the pilots to drop the bombs, but *Apocalypse Now* was at the end of its ragged rope: it needed a concise, merciful ending (just like the war in Vietnam), not forty-five-minute improvs. But Brando had fallen in love with that way of working. It had grown on him ever since he started to have his lines written up on sets or on the costumes of other actors. If filmmaking was so insane, Marlon would be crazy with it. Perhaps those meandering scenes survive somewhere, like snowflakes that decline to melt. But maybe the unstable film stock rotted years ago, along with everything else in that jungle—the chewing gum and the Constitution. Acting a scene for a movie is like betting on a number at roulette—hoping against hope that it will come through the absurd fragmentation. Perhaps one day minutes of these hours will be found, in an attic in Prague or in a former aircraft hangar in Saigon, with this bald, fat man describing the end of the world and the film stock mottled like the wings of irradiated butterflies.

"My name is Ozymandias, king of kings:
Look on my works, ye Mighty, and despair!"
Nothing beside remains. Round the decay
Of that colossal wreck, boundless and bare
The lone and level sands stretch far away.[18]

epilogue

A distant sound is heard, coming as if out of the sky, like the sound
of a string snapping, slowly and sadly dying away. Silence follows,
broken only by the sound of an axe striking a tree in the orchard far
away.

One way to appreciate the thread of acting in what is called ordinary life is to look through someone's photo album. It could
even be your own. There we are in life in what often seems like
a very long run. Day after day, shot after shot, without discern-
ible variation. I suppose this is close to what Thoreau meant by
the life of quiet desperation, with the plod of everyday sounding
like the fall of earth on one's own grave. But the photos are a
treasury, too, a history that brings comfort, and much more. We
see the way we have come and call it a story.

Life gives us our part at the outset, though it is not spelled
out. We don't have a Kazan or a Stanislavsky to instruct us how

to play it. We are on our own and quite soon we feel the restraint or the dismay of its being just one day after another. So it's hardly unexpected or original if sometimes the player self realizes that his or her part is close to being boring. But when he passes the exterior of his theatre, his venue, there is the warning sign, couched in smash-hit glee and neon, "SHOULD RUN FOREVER." Every year, perhaps, like a director touching up a successful show, a doctor comes by and checks out your parts and your performance. "Yes, that's it—I think you've got it now. Try not to overdo it in that revelation scene. Don't worry. You'll be dead in the long run."

The notion of the long run is the culmination to the idea of rehearsal. Outsiders often think of theatre as a paradise of rehearsal in which the play gradually comes to life. Sometimes it can be more rewarding to watch rehearsals than to see a finished performance. Rehearsing a play is a series of problems, arguments, and failures, but it is a paradise. It is not just that people learn their lines and their blocking. They come to understand the needs and rhythms of their fellows. They begin to perceive a unified philosophy or tone to a production, and to all production. One consequence of rehearsals like these—six weeks, eight weeks, twelve?—is to think of a theatre company as an ensemble, a group of players who will grow together in a common attitude to theatre. It is a beautiful notion, not just aesthetic but close to politics. It has had examples in the Moscow Arts Theatre, the Berliner Ensemble, the Group Theater, the old movie studio system, and the teams that make television shows like *The Sopranos*. Countless plays and productions have depended on it—just as a playwright will often learn how to improve his play by watching rehearsals.

But there are great plays about people who never meet until they do so on stage: Romeo sees Juliet; Blanche meets Stanley; Annie Sullivan comes to take care of Helen Keller. The moment of strangeness is vital in those situations, and it may be dulled in ensemble familiarity and the idea that we had done it a hundred times in rehearsal.

The making of movies discovered a precious immediacy and its energy in those unexpected collisions. And so there has grown up in movies the idea that rehearsal can undermine the now of it all. So some actors like "to go for it," not just without preparation, or meeting, but with as few takes as possible. Of course, this strategy owes something to the way most movies cannot afford the time for rehearsal.

Immediacy cannot be denied. You met your future spouse just once and it was then or never. In plenty of ways, important things—dramatic things—do happen "at first sight." So there is a battle in acting between the treasured first time and getting a good thing right. It is a mirror image of the regular dilemma in life between freshness and habit.

The long run. *A Streetcar Named Desire* ran for 855 performances on Broadway. Eight hundred fifty-five times to smash the tableware or scoop up the ruined Blanche as if you've just thought of it. Eight hundred fifty-five times to step forward for the ovation. Eight hundred fifty-five times living in that drab place in Elysian Fields. Brando had his own routine for getting through the grind: $550 a week and several girls in his dressing room every evening. That was a life of abandon such as Stanley would never have dared. The actor missed a few performances when his face got battered in a fight, and Anthony Quinn stepped in. Yet there are some actors who become as desperate as Barrymore with the repetition. They see the playmaking process as an arc: months of preparation, a few weeks of playing at their peak, and then the long decline of hating yourself for doing the same thing every night until it seems stupid. Life knows that dismay. There are wives who come home after work and find the men waiting for dinner. They cook it, and the men consume it in silence. And then one day the wife never comes home. In his lifetime Yul Brynner played *The King and I* 4,625 times. He did other plays and movies. He was married four times. But if he ever walked into a room, the people there saw the King, and they were flummoxed if he had hair.

Which number performance did you see? It could be daunting to have to do it so often, yet you never met anyone who was disappointed by Brynner, and there are repetitions that never stale. In his lifetime Brando must have gone beyond five thousand sexual hits, and I'm sure some were better than others (for him, and for the partners). But he never seems to have been sorry for himself because of that. I think he kept trying.

But in the photo album, we can see a person at different points of her life. We see the inroad on life we miss if we are with her nearly every day. We see the changes and her mixture of loss and endurance. And one of the signifiers in movie careers is exactly that: the inescapable revelation of aging and alteration.

So it happened in the process of doing this book that I looked again at *Pretty Woman* a few days before I saw *August: Osage County* at a movie theatre. Neither of those films is near what I regard as great. Without having seen the Tracy Letts play on stage, I am prepared to concede that the film of *August: Osage County* is a mess and a spoilage, with some good acting but many more problems. As for *Pretty Woman*—which I have probably seen five or six times over the years—it is a shameless fantasy about a prostitute made into a princess with an unalleviated adoration of shopping. The scenes where Vivien goes to Rodeo Drive are like thick, rich cream. You shouldn't be watching them, but you can't stop. Julia Roberts was, from the outset, a star; she was pretty—she became beautiful—but she was gorgeous beyond belief where "gorgeousness" was like a mainline into one's hopeless desires. Her smile ran the risk of obliterating her face. For several years, it was fanciful for her to pretend to normalcy. Her few stage adventures have not been successful, and I doubt that she could do Hedda Gabler or Tracy Lord out in the open.

But her quality as an actress is not quite the point here, just as I feel finally that performance is a more important or generative venture than differences of quality. If acting is an attempt to which most of us are vulnerable in real life, it hardly matters whether we are doing a good or a bad job. When we stand up and lie down, do we do it well, or is it just our way of being?

But it was moving to have Vivien in close-up in my head at the same time as Barbara, her character from *August: Osage County*. Just as she played blancmange soft in *Pretty Woman,* so she was reaching for unexpected severity in *August*. She holds that scattered film together and is either unaware of or unafraid of how hard or epic she looks. She seldom smiles, and her frown is made of sun-beaten ground and being a journey from the ocean. In *Pretty Woman,* she was a kid with a head full of young impulses and a body ready for playful sex. But in *August: Osage County* she has lost faith in those things and much more. In the shift from Los Angeles to rural Oklahoma, she seems to have gone back in time. It is startling and awesome to see how Vivien has become Barbara. She has the burnished look of a pioneer woman who has known a harsh life—the death of a child from cholera, perhaps; the three years when the harvest failed; the time she was lost in the snow and had to have two frostbitten toes amputated; or taking the wrong cutoff. And the bear—she never talks about the bear any more than it remembers her.

As I say, in life we seldom have the chance to notice such shifts in the people we live with, or in ourselves. The long run can erase consciousness. In acting careers the natural drama of growing older and of losing so much is lucid and inescapable. Yet it does not need to be stressed. Quite simply it is there and it is one more reason why acting matters. With our favorite actors we have seen them grow older, and we read the implication that something just as drastic must have happened to us. Acting is an entertainment, but it is a model for our existence and collapse. We try to act human. That seems the least we can do, and as long as that condition prevails—do not trust it forever—then acting is our engine, and we are driving on a desert road.

notes

Epigraph: Opening to the screenplay of *Les Enfants du Paradis* (1943), written by Jacques Prevert, directed by Marcel Carne.

1. It is near the end of *Sophie's Choice* (1979), in Chapter 15, that Sophie reveals to Stingo what happened when a Nazi doctor told her: "You may keep one of your children. The other one will have to go. Which one will you keep?" It is appalling to read just as it must have been hideous to write. In the film, no matter that it is played with terrible dignity, it comes close to being unbearable, or even illegitimate —is such pretending decent? In the book, "Her thought processes dwindled, ceased. Then she felt her legs crumple. 'I can't choose! I can't choose!' She began to scream. Oh, how she recalled her own screams! Tormented angels never screeched so loudly above hell's pandemonium. '*Ich kann nicht wahlen!*' she screamed." She chose her son, but she lost him, too. She never learns what happened to him.

2. The Polish actor played by Jack Benny in Ernst Lubitsch's *To Be or Not to Be*. Whenever Tura begins the soliloquy, "To be or . . .," a handsome uniformed officer gets up and leaves his seat in the theater—to make a rendezvous with Tura's wife (Carole Lombard). But how can a conscientious Hamlet protect his own romantic life?

3. See Bob Thomas, *Golden Boy: The Untold Story of William Holden* (1983).

4. See David Richards, *Played Out: The Jean Seberg Story* (1981), ix–xi.

5. See Francis Phippen, *Authentic Memoirs of Edmund Kean* (1814); Harold Newcomb Hillebrand, *Edmund Kean* (1933).

6. Samuel Taylor Coleridge, *Table Talk,* April 27, 1823.

7. See Richard Schickel, *D. W. Griffith: An American Life* (1983), 272–309.

8. See Jonathan Croall, *John Gielgud: Matinee Idol to Movie Star* (2011), 260.

9. See Hazlitt, *Morning Chronicle,* January 27, 1814, quoted in *Hazlitt on Theatre* (1957).

10. Screenplay to *Les Enfants du Paradis.*

11. Jean-Paul Sartre, *Kean* (1954).

12. Tynan, *The Observer,* May 12, 1956.

13. Arthur Miller, *Timebends: A Life* (1987), 416.

14. *My Lunches with Orson,* conversations between Orson Welles and Henry Jaglom (2013), 136.

15. Miller, *Timebends,* 182.

16. See Terry Coleman, *Olivier* (2005); Laurence Olivier, *Confessions of an Actor* (1982); Alexander Walker, *Vivien: The Life of Vivien Leigh* (1987).

17. See Barry Paris, *Garbo* (1995), 295–96; and Olivier, *Confessions of an Actor,* 92, where he recounts an attempt to warm up the great lady that ended with her throttled sigh, "Oh vell, live'sh a pain anyway," which suggests that he could impersonate her better than she could him. In the matter of posterity's version, that talent can be crucial.

18. Elia Kazan, *A Life* (1988), 143–44.

19. Olivier, *Confessions of an Actor,* 20.

20. See Coleman, *Olivier,* 265.

21. Ibid., 131–32.

22. Coleman, *Olivier,* 287. In his *Confessions,* Olivier refers to that affair without naming Tutin. In fact, Leigh had to be escorted away from stage rehearsals for *The Entertainer* for causing a disturbance over the matter.

23. Richard Eyre, *Utopia and Other Places* (1993), 199.

24. See Matt Trueman, "Did Daniel Day-Lewis See His Father's Ghost as Hamlet?" *The Guardian,* October 29, 2012.

25. Olivier, *Confessions of an Actor,* 102.

26. Coleman, *Olivier,* 313–14.

27. Donald Spoto, *Laurence Olivier: A Biography* (1992), 309.

28. Coleman, *Olivier,* 313.

ACT II. TWILIGHT

Epigraph: Stage direction for act 1, scene 1 of *Table Manners* (1973), by Alan Ayckbourn, the first part of *The Norman Conquests.*

1. Stephen Sondheim, *Look, I Made a Hat* (2011), 156.

2. See Croall, *John Gielgud,* 466–71.

3. See Alan Kendall, *David Garrick: A Biography* (1955).

4. See Marlon Brando, *Songs My Mother Taught Me* (1994); Peter Manso, *Brando: The Biography* (1994).

5. Mark Amory, transcripts for an Olivier biography never written, quoted in Coleman, *Olivier,* 63.

6. See Gene Fowler, *Good Night, Sweet Prince* (1944); Margot Peters, *The House of Barrymore* (1990).

7. See Orson Welles and Peter Bogdanovich, *This Is Orson Welles* (1992), 25. There's no doubt that Welles adored Barrymore, and cherished stories about him. But in *My Lunches with Orson,* he admits that he suspects Barrymore was clinically insane, 260. The plot theme of someone acting crazy or "eccentric," sometimes to stave off the real threat, is as rich as they come. Moreover, in life itself, actors have a special license for acting deranged.

8. See Fowler, *Good Night, Sweet Prince,* 460–68. Also, Mary Astor, *My Story* (1959) 74. But then recollect a Welles story in which, on live radio, a teasing Barrymore introduced Welles as the bastard son of his sister Ethel and the pope. It's as if the theme of illegitimacy was a comic pattern in Barrymore's mind.

9. As a writer, John le Carré is bound up in subterfuges that begin in espionage but which find their own theatre. He was the son of a confidence trickster and a liar (made into fiction in *A Perfect Spy,* 1986). He has a half-sister, Charlotte Cornwell, who is an actress. In *The Little Drummer Girl* (1983), the heroine is a left-wing actress who owes a little to Vanessa Redgrave—though Diane Keaton took the part in the film. Above all, le Carré has happily conspired in the notion that the British secret service has been a club and a school for actors. No one fulfilled (and betrayed) that club more than Kim Philby. But in the two screen versions of *Tinker Tailor Soldier Spy* (one with Alec Guinness as George Smiley, the other with Gary Oldman), le Carré has helped us see how far espionage is a play in development.

10. Croall, *John Gielgud,* 393.

11. See Barry Paris, *Louise Brooks* (1989); Louise Brooks, *Lulu in Hollywood* (1982).

12. Interview with Daniel Taradash, *Backstory 2: Interviews with Screenwriters of the 1940s and 1950s* (1991), 325.

13. The memoirs and legends of the Studio are myriad, and there is the television program *Inside the Actors Studio,* which admits people who have never been inside. So the Studio is a state of mind now. But there are two useful books: Foster Hirsch, *A Method to Their Madness: The History of the Actors Studio* (1984); Steven Vineberg, *Method Actors: Three Generations of an American Acting Style* (1994).

14. Kazan, *A Life,* 116–17.

15. Ibid., 63. To read *A Life* is to understand, and share, Kazan's fear and dislike of Strasberg. The teacher was authoritarian, power-hungry, suspicious, and (the largest failure in Kazan's eyes) sexually impeded or

closed. There is a case to be made that Strasberg took over the Studio largely because he was nervous of and unsuited to actual production. This culminates in Kazan's lengthy, relished account of the disaster when Strasberg took his Actors Studio production of *The Three Sisters* to London in 1964.

16. See Konstantin Stanislavsky, *An Actor Prepares* (1936); *An Actor's Work* (1938); *Creating a Role* (1961).

17. Harold Clurman, *The Fervent Years* (1945), 43.

18. Peters, *The House of Barrymore*, 233.

19. Clurman, *The Fervent Years*, 216. Clurman made the point that the novelty and panache of the Mercury on stage did not mask the essential safety of its work. So one has to say that on radio and film Welles would be far more dangerous—in the best sense. *Citizen Kane* is more subversive than any American play of its era.

20. See Kazan, *A Life*, 300–301.

21. Ibid.

22. Ibid., 66.

23. Tennessee Williams, *A Streetcar Named Desire* (1947), scene 4.

24. Selznick, *A Private View* (1983), 298–328.

25. Tennessee Williams to Audrey Wood, *Represented by Audrey Wood* (1981).

26. Kazan, *A Life*, 343.

ACT III. A MOMENT LATER

Epigraph: Screenplay for *Persona* (1966), written and directed by Ingmar Bergman.

1. It has been suggested that the film outlined here has some resemblances to David Cronenberg's *The Dead Zone* (1983). That may be so. However, even its best friend would admit that that film is alarmingly untidy. And the film alluded to here is apparently meant to stand for

the absurd and melodramatic vagaries of the entire process. So a match is hard to pin down. Still, the reader is at liberty to see that film and to wonder whether figures represented on screen by Christopher Walken, Brook Adams, and Colleen Dewhurst are here on the page. Of course, that very casting is itself so far-fetched as to jeopardize the project.

ACT IV. THAT NIGHT

Epigraph: Stage direction for August Strindberg, *Miss Julie* (1888).

1. This passage is from Vladimir Nabokov's *The Real Life of Sebastian Knight* (1941). It is entirely proper that this fine and elusive book has never been attempted for the screen. I have sometimes thought I would like to try it before I die. But it might be simpler to die, or just to describe it as a lost film. Not enough movies exist in that charmed state.

2. See John Miller, *Judi Dench, With a Crack in Her Voice* (1998), 234.

3. Eyre, *Utopia and Other Places,* 98.

4. Michael Freedland, *Peter O'Toole* (1983), 189–227.

5. Sondheim, *Look, I Made a Hat,* 156.

6. See Andre Bazin, *What Is Cinema?* vol. 2 (1971), 47–78. Werner Herzog's cinema is crowded with vivid nonprofessionals: Bruno S in *The Enigma of Kaspar Hauser,* the bears in *Grizzly Man,* and maybe Klaus Kinski in so many films. (Everyone agreed that Kinski behaved unprofessionally.)

7. Robert Bresson, *Notes on Cinematography* (1977), 49, 42.

8. See Erving Goffman, *The Presentation of Self in Everyday Life* (1959), the groundbreaking work in social psychology that compares ordinary behavior with the rhetorical poses and language of theatre. At Bath, in the summer of 2014, I saw Noël Coward's *Hay Fever.* After the short first act, it seemed very conventional: the Bliss family, in Berkshire, have a house full of awkward weekend guests. Judith Bliss is a famous actress, thinking of retirement and comeback. Then in act II the play soars sublimely as the Blisses begin to act out one of Judith's

famous melodramas (*Love's Whirlwind*) to defy and frighten away their visitors. Being with an actress has consumed their chance of real life. *Hay Fever* is very funny, but alarming, too. In the same way, Pirandello's *Six Characters in Search of an Author* is disturbingly serious, yet comic. It's the story of a cast looking for their play. The two works were written just a few years apart (1921–24), which suggests how the structures of drama were beginning to run our real show.

9. Claire Bloom, *Limelight and After: The Education of an Actress* (1982), 174–75.

10. Henry James to Henrietta Reubell, December 31, 1894, *A Life in Letters,* ed. Philip Horne (1999), 272.

11. Ibid., 274.

12. James to Robert Underwood Johnson, June 24, 1895, ibid., 282.

13. Brando, *Songs My Mother Taught Me,* 4.

14. Olivier, *Confessions of an Actor,* 20.

15. Ibid., 145.

16. Brando would not share his body with Maria Schneider, but he could be a superbly physical actor. His shyness on *Last Tango* gets at a fascinating confusion of a character's body and the actor's. See my "Sinister Cinema" (on left-handedness), *Sight and Sound,* August 2014. Then consider David Fincher in the same magazine, October 2014, saying that he cast Rosamund Pike in *Gone Girl* because the actress was an only child—are such things visible? (She is also the child of two opera singers—can you hear it?)

17. Brando, *Songs My Mother Taught Me,* 430–31.

18. Percy Bysshe Shelley, "Ozymandias" (1818).

EPILOGUE

Epigraph: Stage direction for *The Cherry Orchard* (1904) by Anton Chekhov.

acknowledgments

The Yale series Why X Matters is a mark of the initiative as well as the distinction of the press. For the thing in question does matter, but the form of the title, first, and then the book allow for a discursive conversational approach just because the task of justification is so far beyond reach that it doesn't really matter. So I'll always be grateful that my old friend Steve Wasserman, an editor at the press, wondered whether I would like to take on acting. His enthusiasm for the venture and his resolve to publish it with wit and panache have been sources of encouragement. Not many conventional publishers are as lively as Yale University Press at the moment.

The book that has resulted owes thanks in many places: to my father, who usually acted, and sometimes on stage; to my school and its belief in the Elizabethan actor Edward Alleyn; and to the several people who have stimulated my interest in acting, and been able to talk about it. That list includes Alan Badel,

Irene Selznick, Bob Gottlieb, Jim Toback, Steven Bach, Mark Feeney, Douglas McGrath, Peter Smith, and Michael Barker, all of whom in one way or another understood that acting was a difficult professional pursuit and a constant amateur preoccupation. The book is dedicated to five people with whom I was involved for a time in putting on plays: it may have been the happiest time of my life.

The book was assisted and enriched by the comments of Richard Eyre at a crucial moment. Steve Wasserman passed the text on for copyediting to Dan Heaton. Working with Dan was a pleasure and an education, and the first indication I had that if acting does matter, the book might be enjoyable. (That he turned out to be an Arsenal supporter brought a welcome, disputatious spice to our conversation.) I am also very appreciative of the design, and especially the cover, as delivered by Sonia Shannon.

David Thomson was born in south London, as bombs were falling. He survived and attended Dulwich College, one of the very few schools in the world founded by an actor. From there he went on to the London School of Film Technique and a rather overdone obsession with movies that was barely rescued by his career as a celebrity podiatrist. Between soles and toes, he assembled the *Biographical Dictionary of Film* and several other books on cinema. Unusually prone to boredom (or its act), he also conceived and wrote strange books on the lives and works of Warren Beatty and Nicole Kidman and a legendary study on Nevada, as well as a few novels—*A Bowl of Eggs, Suspects,* and *Silver Light*—though the label "novel" was disputed. Retired now from feet, he is movie critic for the *New Republic,* a researcher on left-handedness, and the father of five extraordinary children. He is no longer accepting patients.